RECEIVE THE TRUTH!

RECEIVE THE TRUTH!

A collection of
Twenty Questions and Ten Bible Talks
focusing on key issues in contemporary
Christian-Jewish relations
and Christian spirituality

Alex Jacob

The Church's Ministry among Jewish People (CMJ)

Glory to Glory Publications

First published in Great Britain by
Glory to Glory Publications
an imprint of
Buy Research Ltd.

ISBN 978-0-9567831-0-3

Printed in Great Britain
by
CPI Mackays Ltd.

Contents

TWENTY QUESTIONS

The range of questions below are all genuine questions that I have been asked in my teaching role with the Church's Ministry among Jewish People (CMJ) over the past few years. Most of the questions were asked during discussion meetings or at teaching events. Some however, were submitted in writing or by e-mail. I have reworked some of them in order to form composite questions with the aim of reflecting the range of questions being asked on a similar theme.

TEN BIBLE TALKS

The range of Bible talks below are ones that in my experience are key and foundational scriptures throwing light upon humankind's condition, God's saving election of the Hebrew people, and God's extension of that saving election amongst the entirety of humankind. Accordingly, a reflection on these key texts will assist immeasurably our ability to discern God's redemptive purposes and how the Hebrew dynamic continues to be an inescapable part of that redemptive plan. Please do not expect these short talks, however, to answer all your questions! Consider them rather as a departure point in your quest to explore the wonders of God's redemptive plan.

Note on Bible References

The name given is the book in the Bible, the first number refers to the chapter, and the following number or numbers refer to the verses. So Romans 1:1-16 is referring to Romans, chapter 1 and verses 1 to 16. All Bible references, unless otherwise stated, are taken from the New International Version (NIV).

Dedication

I dedicate this book to the memory of Kristine Luken who served with me at CMJ and helped in the early stages of its composition.

Kristine was tragically murdered in Israel in 2010.

Kristine Luken
1966 – 2010

Acknowledgements

I would like to thank all who have helped shape my thinking, preaching, teaching and writing over the years. I would especially like to thank my colleagues within CMJ (The Church's Ministry among Jewish People), my immediate family, Mandy, Luke, Emily and Ben, and the publishing team at Glory to Glory. Your support, encouragement, humour, wisdom and prayerfulness have been a great blessing.

If I stand, Lord, let me stand on the promise that you will pull me through — and if I can't, let me fall on the grace that first brought me to you.

Introduction

This book has emerged in part, as a follow up to my first book in the field of Jewish-Christian relations (*The Case for Enlargement Theology*) in the sense that many people requested a more concise work at an introductory level. I hope *Receive the Truth!* achieves this and will help many people to gain a better initial understanding of key issues within contemporary Jewish-Christian relations.

The title may appear to be a somewhat arrogant one. However, the term comes from a prayer, itself based in part on Colossians 2:3, attributed to John Calvin (1509-1564) and used by some of the early Reformers:

> Heavenly Father, in Your Son Jesus Christ is hidden all the treasures of wisdom and knowledge. Touch our hearts and our minds by Your Holy Spirit and give to each one reverence and humility, for without these gifts it is impossible to receive the truth. *Amen*.

I have prayed this prayer regularly during my preaching ministry as I think it has a beautiful biblical rhythm. The prayer affirms God is Father, Son and Holy Spirit, and that in Jesus we will find the treasure we long for. However, we cannot receive this treasure by our own efforts alone; we need the touch of the Holy Spirit and his gifts of reverence and humility. These gifts appear sadly lacking in many aspects of contemporary living and in some aspects of so-called Christian theology.

I hope this book may become a useful resource to many and will in some way guide you in the search for truth.

Twenty Questions and Answers

Question 1
Has not God finished with Israel? Surely God is doing 'a new thing' today with the church?

God is a promise-keeping God. The promises to Israel cannot be revoked or transferred to the church (or any other entity), without distorting or undermining God's faithfulness. I understand that God remains faithful to Israel. This can be seen partly in the restoring of Israel as a nation and partly in terms of significant numbers of Jewish people discovering and responding to the truth about Jesus. While proclaiming God's everlasting love for Israel, there is also the sense that through the person and work of Jesus and the mission of the church, God is indeed doing a 'new thing'. Yet this 'new thing' does not sever Israel from God's promises or purposes, but rather this 'new thing' should be understood as both a fulfilling and an enlargement of God's covenantal promises to Israel and God's intention to bless all of His creation. This promise of blessing beyond Israel, yet through Israel, was originally given in Genesis 12:3.

I offer two clear convictions, one negative and one positive, about God's dealings with Israel and the church: **no**, God has not finished with Israel; and **yes**, God is doing a new thing with the church. A correct reading of the Bible means these two statements are not contradictory but are complementary within God's overall purposes.

Question 2

In supporting Israel, are you not taking sides and denying the legitimate rights of Palestinians?

The question itself surely needs a gentle challenge: in not supporting Israel or in supporting the Palestinians, are you in fact taking sides? It seems to be very difficult and perhaps unhelpful to adopt a truly dispassionate or a neutral position as regards this whole subject. Neither CMJ nor the author take a simplistic or polarised stance in a tremendously complex area which is so deeply rooted in areas of theology, history, politics and economics.

CMJ believes the establishing of a safe homeland for Jewish people is part of the fulfilment of God's purposes and promises for all of creation. After nearly 2000 years of Jewish exile and anti-Semitism, culminating in the horrors of the Holocaust, we stand and rejoice with Israel in her right to exist within secure and peaceful boundaries. We reject all forms of terrorism and actively strive to seek a peaceful and just solution to the human and political rights of all peoples.

In supporting Israel (its right to exist, its right to exist in peace and within secure borders and affirming Israel's continuing role within God's purpose for humankind) we do not believe that Israel is above criticism and we call upon Israel to live out her biblical ethical demands, in terms of just treatment of Palestinians. Equally, we would call upon all to recognise Israel's right to exist within secure and peaceful boundaries. On a local level CMJ continues to work tirelessly in attempting to model reconciliation between Jews and Arabs. The ultimate peace and justice we all long for can only be fully established when all have responded to the liberating and reconciling power of the gospel.

For further study see the *CMJ Statement on Israel and the Palestinians* (reproduced below, p103).

Question 3

In seeing the modern restoration of Israel as a direct fulfilment of Scripture, are you not taking a very literal and biased view of Scripture?

No, I believe the way CMJ interprets and applies the key biblical texts follows the very best practice of evangelical Christian biblical teaching. CMJ, while recognising the use of symbolism, poetry, typology and the multi-faceted nature and historical contexts of much prophecy, believes that texts should be interpreted by their plain meaning, rather than pursuing a more deductive or over- spiritualised hermeneutic.[1] CMJ upholds and champions the view that God's character is verifiable through the outworking of history, which includes the modern restoration of Israel.

For further study on how to interpret the Bible see my book *The Case for Enlargement Theology* (Chapter 4).

Question 4

In teaching the importance of Jewish evangelism today, are you not in danger of undermining good Jewish-Christian relations?

Sharing the gospel sensitively and appropriately with Jewish people is at the very heart of CMJ. We realise that some within the field of Jewish-Christian relations argue against Jewish evangelism and see such attempts by Christians as theologically inappropriate. CMJ does not endorse this view, but rather sees the theological priority of Jewish evangelism (Romans 1:16). In sharing the gospel with Jewish people, we are challenging Jewish myths and fears about Jesus, especially the following:

(a) Jesus is 'not really Jewish', and to study his life and claims is not acceptable Jewish research;

(b) Jewish people will somehow come to harm if they encounter the Christian gospel; and

(c) Believing in Jesus results in a cessation of true Jewish identity.

In challenging these views, we believe we are not undermining Jewish-Christian relations, but rather we are contributing to deeper and more meaningful dialogue, in a robust and respectful way.

For further study see also the Bible talk on Romans 1:1-16 in this book.

Question 5

Does your concern for and focus upon Jewish people undermine the church's work within Islamic settings?

No, in fact the opposite is true. CMJ believes that the cultural and theological insights which have been gained over the past 200 years from sharing the gospel with Jewish people actually contribute to and complement evangelistic work within an Islamic setting. In fact, there is a lot of common ground between elements of Jewish cultural and religious life and many elements of Islamic cultural and religious life. This is discovered when those working evangelistically within Jewish or Islamic contexts share insights about their work and they become aware it is in fact complementary insights that are being shared. For example, Martin Goldsmith (a Jewish believer in Jesus) has worked evangelistically for many years within Islamic settings and he concludes his reflections on how Muslims have become Christians: 'Muslim converts have these three things in common – a long term relationship or friendship with a Christian whom they respect, a serious reading of at least part of the New Testament and an experience of a miracle which they associate with Jesus Christ and the Christian faith.'[2] The three things identified in that passage have frequently been affirmed by others working within a Jewish evangelistic setting.

A final point that is also worth highlighting is the one key theological truth which is at the heart of CMJ. It is that God has not replaced Israel/Jewish people with the church and Gentile people. In other words, God is faithful and this does not allow for us to adopt a 'replacement model' when proclaiming the gospel or speaking of the purpose and identity of the church. This is important in terms of engagement with Islamic teachers, for Islam is based on a replacement model – namely their claim that Mohammad brings the final revelation of God which replaces or completes the partial previous revelations given to Israel, and later to the church through Jesus. If as Christians we also adopt a replacement model (thinking that the message of Jesus implies that Israel has been replaced because of Israel's failure to live up to her calling), then we have a weaker foundation in arguing against Islamic replacement concepts. As Christians, our security/identity is not based on our 'spiritual performance' or upon our replacing Israel, but rather on the truth that Israel's security/identity and our security/identity are based upon the one truth of God's grace demonstrated primarily through his covenantal faithfulness. This *faithfulness* needs to be proclaimed within every context – including the Islamic – and it is the faithfulness of the God of Israel, the God of Abraham, Isaac and Jacob.

Question 6

I am a Jewish man, but I have not found any spiritual connection with G-d. My question is: How do I find the Messiah and how can someone Jewish connect with G-d? I feel there is something missing in my life.

You have raised a very important question (maybe the most important question of all!) about finding and sustaining a living relationship with G-d.

Clearly, each person has a unique personality and unique life experiences. Yet as a Christian, despite the rich diversity of human existence, I believe there is only 'one way' for all people (Jewish and Gentile) to fully encounter G-d and to know the peace and purpose that only G-d can give. It seems to me from your e-mail you are already moving towards discovering the 'one way'; clearly you have a sense of the need for an 'emotional connection' with G-d; you appear to have reflected deeply upon your Jewish identity and the issues around the purpose of life. I think such longings and reflections lie deep within every human heart. I guess in part this is what it means to be made in the image of G-d. Maybe such longings are especially poignant within Jewish people as Jewish religious heritage makes people more aware of God's great concern for his sin-ravaged creation and for our own brokenness and helplessness?

This 'one way' is the way of Jesus (*Yeshua*). I assume the first key question then is: who is Jesus? The answer is found primarily within the pages of the New Testament (this is a Jewish book written mainly by Jewish writers about a Jewish man). Within this book we read of the man Jesus. We discover so much about his birth, life, teaching and relationships. We discover Jesus lived a perfect life and fulfilled the Torah completely, something no other person before or since has been able to come close to.

The New Testament also tells of his sacrificial death and his victorious rising from the dead. One such New Testament description of this reality is given by a once-sceptical Rabbi, who had violently opposed those (initially nearly all the believers in Jesus were Jewish) who came to believe in Jesus as the Messiah of Israel and Lord of all. This Rabbi states,

For what I received I passed on to you as of first importance: that Christ [Messiah] *died for our sins according to the Scriptures, and that he was buried, and that he rose again on the third day according to the Scriptures, and that he appeared to Peter, and then to the Twelve. After that he appeared to more than five hundred of the brothers at the same time, most of whom are still living, though some have fallen asleep. Then he appeared to James, then to all of the apostles, and last of all he appeared to me also, as to one abnormally born.*

1 Corinthians 15:3-8

The New Testament presents a clear and wonderful picture of Jesus. We are given a choice! Ultimately all must decide whether to accept Jesus as Messiah and Lord, or to reject such an understanding of him. In accepting him, we need to take some key steps: Firstly, we need to confess to God that we are sinners and have fallen short of God's ways. Secondly, we seek G-d's forgiveness and his renewal of our lives. Thirdly, we commit ourselves to following and trusting Jesus for the rest of our lives. This process can begin right now for you in the quietness and privacy of your own prayer to G-d, in the name of Jesus. However, for this process to strengthen and mature it becomes important wherever possible to make this private prayer a public declaration and to link with a supportive Christian or Messianic Jewish community/church/congregation – a community where you can build trusted friendships, discover more about following/serving Jesus and experience the reality of the Holy Spirit in your daily living.

I want to assure you that in responding to Jesus, you are not in any way denying your Jewish identity. Many followers of Jesus today are both faithful followers of Jesus and faithful to their Jewish identity and inheritance. Clearly there is so much more to say and discuss. I hope if you want to explore some of these issues further you will be able to find a Christian or Messianic Jewish friend you can trust and a welcoming church you can attend. Equally, if you want to contact me again, I would be pleased to hear from you or to meet with you at your convenience, in the strictest confidence.

Question 7

What do you mean by 'Jewish Roots teaching'? If you promote this teaching within the church, are you not adding issues of secondary importance to the church?

Jewish Roots teaching is a teaching that seeks to honour and develop insights from biblical Jewish life and to apply them where appropriate into the wider life of the church. Such insights would include developing a 'Hebraic mindset' rather than a 'Greek dominated way of thinking', referring to Jesus by using his Hebrew name '*Yeshua*', the celebrating of the main biblical Feasts, the valuing of Sabbath and an engagement with Jewish liturgy/music, etc.

In terms of the second part of the question, I believe that Jewish Roots teaching, when appropriately introduced into a local church, helps the church to gain a far greater understanding of central issues. For example, there are many scenes in the Gospel accounts which only begin to reveal their full significance when we understand the essential Jewishness of the characters (including Jesus) and their contexts. Also, for example, the link between Holy Communion and Passover can be truly significant in helping Christians appreciate more fully the redemptive love of God as displayed in these events. I understand rediscovering our biblical Jewish roots brings a foretaste of what Paul calls 'life from the dead' (Romans 11:15). Such teaching has great potential to help the whole church grow in understanding and to renew areas of service, worship and mission.

Clearly any form of teaching can be over-used or presented in an arrogant or aggressive manner which can lead to divisions. Sadly, some Christian 'Jewish Roots teachings' have perhaps fallen into such categories, but where there has been misuse, the best response is seldom non-use, but right use!

Question 8

What is Christian Zionism? Is CMJ part of the Christian Zionist Movement?

Firstly, as is the case with many of these questions (see for example question 15), it is important to define terms. Often terms are extremely potent and somewhat slippery! Who gets to 'define the terms' is an expression of power and status and is very much a current issue within Jewish-Christian relations today. In terms of defining Christian Zionism my simple definition would be: 'a Christian Zionist is a Christian who understands that the events of history leading up to the establishment of Israel as a Jewish state are to be welcomed as a fulfilment of biblical prophecy. Christian Zionists would also seek to give on-going prayerful and practical support to Israel'.

In terms of a more detailed definition I would recommend the one given by Paul Wilkinson in his book *For Zion's Sake*. He defines Christian Zionism as a belief in the following eight areas:

1. A clear biblical distinction between Israel and the church.
2. A pre-tribulation rapture of the church.[3]
3. The full return of the Jewish people to the Land of Israel.
4. Rebuilding of the Temple in Jerusalem.
5. The rise of the antichrist.
6. A seven year period of tribulation.
7. The national salvation of the Jews.
8. The return of Christ to Jerusalem to judge and reign.

In reflecting on these eight points, I personally would want to strongly preach and teach three of them; I would be broadly sympathetic to another four, and I would have some questions about one, namely a pre-tribulation rapture of the church.

Secondly, in defining Christian Zionism, CMJ has stated:

Yes we are Christian Zionists if this means:
1. Standing with the Jewish people as critical friends after almost 2000 years of anti-Semitism.
2. Combating anti-Semitism.
3. Thanking God for the creation and ongoing maintenance of a safe homeland for the Jewish People.
4. Rejoicing in God's faithfulness to the Jewish people.
5. Condemning Palestinian terrorism.
6. Believing the church has not replaced or given up on the Jewish people.

No, CMJ are not Christian Zionists if this means:
1. Ignoring the plight and rights of Palestinians and Israeli Arabs.
2. Believing Israel is above criticism.
3. Ignoring the biblical ethical demands in terms of Israel's treatment of non-Jews.

In reflecting on issues around Zionism, justice and peace I have found the following seven questions and lines of discussion useful:

1. Can we (or should we) talk of human rights without political rights?
2. Is there a meaningful difference between anti-Zionism and anti-Semitism?
3. Does a two state solution or a one state bi-national model seem more creative and helpful in terms of a just settlement within the current Israeli-Palestinian conflict?
4. We need to move beyond the failings of both the 'political right' and the 'political left' in order to seek the wisdom of God's Word.
5. In what way is it more helpful to talk about God's heart for Jewish people, rather than God's heart for Israel?

6. We need to be aware of the growing militant Islamic agenda.

7. A robust rejection of a replacement hermeneutic is a help rather than a hindrance, in our engagement with the claims of Islam.

In terms of the overall view of biblical Zionism, which reflects the general stance of CMJ, the following four points can be affirmed:

1. There has been a physical restoration of Israel. This is a fulfilment of the promises of God.

2. This physical restoration to the Land is a vital link to the future spiritual restoration of Jewish people as they respond to God's call and believe in the gospel. We see signs of this spiritual restoration in terms of the growth of Messianic Jewish congregations and the openness of an increasing number of Jewish people to the gospel.

3. We are in a spiritual battle where a range of forces are seeking to prevent this spiritual restoration.

4. We proclaim this spiritual restoration and renewal will triumph and untold blessings will flow from the physical and spiritual rebirth of Israel.

I hope some of the above is helpful. I know I will spend a lifetime wrestling with some of these issues, and while I wrestle I will pray for a blessing of *shalom* for Jew and Gentile, Israeli and Palestinian, knowing that true *shalom* is only found in Jesus, God's Son, Israel's Messiah and the Saviour of the world, who died and rose, and will return to judge and reign!

Question 9

What is your understanding of Israel as a chosen people?
The understanding of 'a chosen people' is rooted in the
biblical teaching of God's election (calling) of Israel. Moses
sings of Israel as 'the apple of God's eye' (Deuteronomy
32:10) and Israel is declared time and again in the Bible to
have a special/chosen relationship with God (Exodus 4:22;
Jeremiah 31:9; Hosea 11:1; Psalm 105:6).

The term 'Israel' was given to Jacob after he wrestled/
strived with 'God' (Genesis 32:22-32). Later, Jacob's
descendants became known as *bene Yisrael* (sons of Israel).
However, the blessing of Israel predates Jacob and is initially
linked to God's call of Abraham, and his faithful covenantal
promises to Abraham (Genesis 12). These promises are
renewed and enlarged in the subsequent biblical covenants
with Moses and David, and the new covenant with the house
of Israel and the house of Judah (see Jeremiah 31:31-34 and
Hebrews 8).

The understanding of election and covenantal faithfulness
is central to God's purposes and promises. Paul carefully
explores this understanding in Romans 9-11 and affirms that
the gifts and calling of God to Israel are irrevocable (Romans
11:29), and looks forward to the day when all Israel will be
saved (Romans 11:26). Paul understands the promises to
Israel have been confirmed and not revoked in the ministry
of Jesus Christ (see Romans 15:8; 2 Corinthians 1:20).
In the New Testament teaching, Gentiles through faith in
Jesus also become part of the elect of God (Ephesians 1:4;
Ephesians 2:11-22; 1 Peter 1:1). It is also worth exploring that
in the New Testament the term 'Israel' is used in three main
ways: Firstly, It can refer to ethnic Israel (Jacob's physical
descendants); secondly, it can refer to the faithful remnant
within Israel (Romans 9:6 and Romans 11:2-5); thirdly, it can

refer to the church (the community of Jews and Gentiles who love and serve Jesus Christ as Lord). The church is both the called out (*ecclesia*) community (called out from the sin and unbelief of the world to witness and serve God's purposes) and the grafted-in community. The church is grafted into the faithfulness of Israel (see the olive tree teaching in Romans 11) in order to be built into a spiritual people and to serve as a holy priesthood (1 Peter 2:4).

Sadly, ideas about election and those of 'a chosen people' can be misused. It is important to stress that God's election of Israel is primarily a gift for service and witness. Israel is to serve God as a distinctive (holy) community (see Deuteronomy 7:6 and Joel 3:16). This very point is made powerfully by the prophet Isaiah (49:6):

> *"It is too small a thing for you to be my servant*
> *to restore the tribes of Jacob*
> *and bring back those of Israel I have kept.*
> *I will also make you a light for the Gentiles,*
> *that you may bring my salvation to the*
> *ends of the earth."*

As we reflect and explore God's faithful love for Israel and his purposes for the whole of his creation we should be moved to echo Paul's own sense of mystery, awe and joy as expressed in Romans 11:33 and v. 36:

> *Oh the depth of the riches of the wisdom and knowledge*
> *of God!*
> *How unsearchable his judgments,*
> *and his paths beyond tracing out!*
> *. . . For from him and through him and to him*
> *are all things.*
> *To him be the glory forever! Amen.*

Question 10

CMJ is a missionary society; what is your understanding of the mission call today and how is this being promoted by churches?

The call to mission is a natural and appropriate outcome of following Jesus. As Christians grow in becoming 'more like Jesus', the call to be sent out into the world to 'serve and share the gospel' grows within. The words of Jesus, *"Peace be with you! As my Father sent me, I am sending you,"* (John 20:21) begins to shape and challenge the plans and dreams of all active Christians.

At one level, every Christian is a witness to the person and work of Jesus. The words of Peter (1 Peter 3:15-16) give a wonderful sense of purpose, privilege and responsibility to every believer. Regardless of status, age, location or gifting, each has the calling to be a unique witness. However, some Christians have specific callings from God to go and serve in significant ways and within recognised ministries. Paul lists five 'ministries' in Ephesians 4:11 to which Jesus calls Christians (and for which he equips them). In addition, Paul speaks of overseers/elders and deacons in his letters to Timothy and Titus. Paul also sets out the 'qualifications' and requirements for such ministries to flourish (see, for example, 1 Timothy 3 and Titus 1:5-9).

At the heart of hearing God's call to us must be an openness and willingness to obey, alongside the ability to discern needs and opportunities in order to reach out, in the love and grace of Jesus. Such openness and willingness is reflected in the calling of many within the Bible. However, often there is a struggle in coming to terms with God's call. We see this sense of struggle, for example, in the callings of Moses (see Exodus 2:12), Isaiah (see Isaiah 6:1-8) and Jeremiah (see Jeremiah 1:6). The key is that the God who calls is the God who equips. All God's people are being prepared for works of service (Ephesians 4:12); each is encouraged to live a sacrificial life (Romans 12:1-2) and to be open to the gifting of the Holy Spirit (1 Corinthians chapters 12-14) as well as using one's 'natural' abilities and resources in God's work.

In seeking to respond to God's call, it is important to try to examine our motives for doing so. Sadly, baser human motives (such as pride, fame, need for affirmation, etc.) sometimes can distort or even block God's call. In the person of Jesus we see the perfect example of responding to the call of God. Jesus serves in the power of the Holy Spirit. He reaches out in love; he desires to bless those to whom he ministers (see, for example, Matthew 8:3 and v. 7), and he learns to focus upon his Father's perfect will (Matthew 26:39). In response to the ministry and mission of Jesus, Christians both individually and as part of a mission-focused community (the church), seek to put into practice the Great Commission Jesus gives:

"Therefore go and make disciples of all nations, baptising them in the name of the Father and of the Son and of the Holy Spirit, and teaching them to obey everything I have commanded you. And surely I am with you always, to the very end of the age."

Matthew 28:19-20

Question 11

Why is it important to see Jesus in his historical Jewish context?

It is important because the Christian faith is rooted in history. Often people misunderstand the basis for Christianity, for they see the Christian faith as being based primarily upon religious ideas, universal philosophical values or spiritual speculations. This is not the case. Christianity stands or falls upon real historical events rooted in specific places and involving specific communities and individuals. That seems to be why critics of Christianity expend so much effort in trying to undermine the historicity of the New Testament. At the heart of all of this is the person of Jesus.

The witness of Scripture is that this Jesus was born in Bethlehem at a time when the Land of Israel was under Roman control during the reign of the Roman Emperor Caesar Augustus (31 BC – 14 AD). He was circumcised on the eighth day and presented to the Lord at the Temple in Jerusalem. Shortly afterwards, with his family he fled to Egypt before returning to be brought up in Nazareth. Here he grew up in a Jewish context of family, Torah, Synagogue, Scripture and Temple. He taught with a powerful focus upon the kingdom of God. He engaged with the Jewish groupings of his day, bringing out the truth of God's Word and declaring God's saving purposes. In all things he lived a holy life, full of the Holy Spirit. He was often called 'rabbi' and his manners, message and methods all fitted into the wider context of the Jewish world. Later, he was arrested and put to death under Pontius Pilate, he was buried in a borrowed tomb and he was raised to life. Through his atoning death and glorious resurrection, Christians declare Jesus has conquered the power of sin and death. His initial disciples were Jewish people who gathered daily in the Temple courts in Jerusalem and they shared together in their homes, praising God, and being built up and transformed by the Holy Spirit into a community of those focused upon proclaiming and serving Jesus as Lord.

All of this is part of giving an historical context. If our knowledge about Jesus and understanding of his message is to deepen, and our love for him is to mature, then time spent in studying and reflecting upon Jesus in his historical Jewish context is a vital part of discipleship. Indeed it is an act of worship.

For further study I would recommend the writings of N.T. Wright, especially his series on Christian origins and the question of God. In volume 1 of this epic work he states:

> Pontius Pilate belongs in the Creed; (this shows) that the events which are central to Christian belief and life are not reducible to terms of non-spatio-temporal reality, but have to do with events that occurred within the real world. The rootedness of Christianity in history is not negotiable....

Question 12

Sharing the gospel with Jewish people is at the heart of CMJ. Why is this? And how do you go about doing this?

CMJ (The Church's Ministry among Jewish People) was established in 1809 and has always had a clear evangelistic focus in sharing the gospel sensitively and appropriately with Jewish people. Why and how do we go about doing this?

Firstly, we need to have a clear theological framework for Jewish evangelism.

CMJ would argue that sharing the gospel with Jewish people is an absolute priority within the mission calling of the church, as Romans 1:16 states: *'to the Jew first.'* If the church wants to have a clear biblical evangelistic mission for the world, it must firstly engage with the Jewish community. Alongside this priority comes the theological rejection of other theological models of Jewish engagement, namely Replacement Theology (Supersessionism) and Two (Dual) Covenant Theology. CMJ argues that these two models undermine Jewish evangelism. In addition to developing a coherent biblical framework in contrast to either Replacement Theology or Two-Covenant Theology, there is within the mindset of CMJ a clear understanding that God remains faithful to Israel. This faithfulness is seen partly in the recent restoration of Israel as a nation (the promises of the Land made initially in the Abrahamic covenant remain valid, they have not been revoked or transferred to the church) and in the recent growth of the Messianic Jewish movement (Jews who believe in Jesus (*Yeshua*) and remain faithful to their Jewish identity). Therefore, in the work of CMJ there has been, and still is, a supportive practical attitude to Israel. For example, the first 'modern' school, hospital and Protestant church built in Jerusalem were all the result of the work of CMJ. Also, CMJ has always sought to support the emerging

Messianic Jewish movement. For example, a Messianic Jewish community meets in the CMJ church in Jerusalem and another community has sole use of our mission buildings in Tel Aviv. CMJ believes the Jewish hopes outlined in the Torah, Prophets and wisdom literature all point to and find their fulfilment in the person and work of Jesus (the Jewish Messiah and Lord of all). For a Jewish person to become a disciple of Jesus is in no way a denial or rejection of Jewish identity/destiny, but a renewal and fulfilment of the God-given identity/destiny.

Secondly, we need to establish meaningful links with Jewish people. This has been done and continues to be done through our support of Jewish people in Israel (beginning in the 1840s during the Ottoman period, through to the British Mandate and on into the modern state of Israel). Also, similar work of a practical and evangelistic nature was carried out through numerous Mission Centres throughout Eastern Europe (most of this work was terminated as a result of the Holocaust having devastated Jewish communities in the 1940s and the subsequent fall of the communist 'iron curtain' across Europe for fifty years), North Africa and Ethiopia. In the UK the work began with much 'social care work' alongside evangelistic mission based mainly with the very poor Jewish immigrant communities in the East End of London. This work continues to this day in the UK. CMJ employ full-time evangelists who work closely with supportive churches in Jewish areas, Messianic congregations and other mission groups. These evangelistic workers reach out to Jewish people through street outreach, literature distribution and personal contacts. In addition, CMJ believes that such evangelist work both in Israel and the UK needs to be enhanced and supported by an educational program in which Christians can be taught more about the vital Jewish roots of the Christian faith, the horrors of anti-Semitism (which has gained some of its vigour and corrosiveness from Replacement Theology), the importance of the Messianic Jewish movement and God's ongoing faithfulness to his covenant with Abraham, Moses and David.

Thirdly, we need to have a good evangelism strategy underpinned by prayer and faithful financial giving. As stated, we currently have a strategy in the UK with a small team of evangelists and a broad network of prayerful supporters and faithful givers. In order, therefore, to present and sustain a helpful and attractive view of Jesus (*Yeshua*) to Jewish people we need to have these three major components in place. CMJ believes it is able to present and sustain an effective, culturally sensitive and biblically astute Christian apologetic to a wide range of Jewish people.

For further study I encourage readers to dig deeply into Romans 9-11 as this is the key text in many aspects of Jewish-Christian relations. In terms of wider reading there is a huge amount, but I would suggest the following as a good starting point: *Messianic Jews* by John Fieldsend, *Defending Christian Zionism* by David Pawson, *The God of Israel and Christian Theology* by R Kendall Soulen and *The Covenant with the Jews* by Walter Riggans. See Bibliography below for a full list.

Question 13

I am hoping to work one day with a Christian group reaching out to Jewish people. How best should I prepare for this?

I am delighted to hear of the calling you have identified to minister to Jewish people. I believe this is a key calling of the church (Romans 1:16). In terms of preparation I would suggest the following four lines to explore.

Firstly, try to make contact with various Christian organisations (most have good websites) working in Jewish ministry. There are a number of biblically focused and well-established ministries. Each ministry has its own nuanced position and flavour, yet there is much common ground and common work between us. As I work with CMJ (The Church's Ministry among Jewish People), I would suggest you start with us! In addition, look at the excellent work of the following groups/ministries: The Messianic Testimony, Jews for Jesus, Christian Witness to Israel, Bridges for Peace, Christian Friends of Israel, The British Messianic Jewish Alliance, etc. Each of these ministries will hold an annual conference which provides a good opportunity to network with staff and supporters and to connect with and gain the 'flavour' of the ongoing work.

Secondly, invest in study on a personal level. There are a range of books which would be most worthwhile. I outline below a few to start with, which I have valued: *Messianic Jews* by John Fieldsend; *Jewish Identity and Faith in Jesus*, edited by Kai Kjaer-Hansen; *Father Forgive Us* by Fred Wright; *The God of Israel and Christian Theology* by R Kendall Soulen; *The Unusual Suspects* by Richard Gibson, and *For the Love of Zion* by Kelvin Crombie. See Bibliography for full details.

In addition to some great books, there are a number of Bible colleges offering a range of courses in the field of

Jewish-Christian relations. All Nations College has pioneered an MA in Messianic Jewish studies. Also, the Centre for Jewish–Christian Relations at Cambridge (Wesley House) has a useful range of courses.

It may also be worth considering investing some time in Hebrew language studies (Biblical and/or Modern Hebrew).

Thirdly, spend time trying to build friendships and genuine social contacts with Jewish people, as you continue to pray and reflect upon your calling.

Fourthly, and above all, focus upon and draw close to Jesus. Jesus is our model for reaching out to Jewish people. Jesus provides a mission pattern from which we must learn. While, clearly, there is an immense gulf between us and Jesus, as the one and only incarnate Son of God, nevertheless he is the one we seek to emulate in preparing for and doing ministry. Every aspect of his life, especially his understanding of Scripture, his skill at communication, his gentleness yet directness in answering controversial questions, his dependency on his Father's will along with his openness to the Holy Spirit, inspires, humbles and renews us. Focusing upon Jesus and drawing close to him is the best preparation for reaching out to Jewish people. Yet it must also be noted that this 'preparation' is never complete, as the task of learning from Jesus is an ongoing task that continues throughout our lives.

Question 14

I am hoping to talk with a Jewish friend about the deity of Jesus. How should I go about doing this in a helpful way?

I think in all such conversations, we need to sense the prompting of the Holy Spirit in initiating conversations, rather than perhaps forcing our agenda upon others. As 1 Peter 3:15 reminds us, it is often better to respond to the genuine questions our friends and contacts are asking rather than to set our own convictions and insights. Jewish friends often have specific questions and issues around history, identity and theology which we must try to faithfully respond to, with a Holy Spirit inspired mix of robustness and gentleness.

In terms of the issue of the deity of Jesus, I think I would want to start this huge subject by trying to show that the *Shema* (Deuteronomy 6:4), which is at the very heart of Jewish identity, does not undermine a proper Christian understanding of the Trinity, which includes the deity of Jesus. The term 'one' (*ehad* in Hebrew) does not necessarily refer to simple singularity, it can be seen to point to 'a unity in plurality', as in the case of a husband and wife being described as *one* flesh: or a group of people being in *one* mind with regard to a particular action.

Also, I would want to emphasise that the early church (made up in the earliest period exclusively of Jewish people who were steeped in monotheism) quickly came to realise through a range of experiences, such as the resurrection of Jesus and the ongoing ministry of the Holy Spirit, that Jesus is Lord – which they declared. This early Christian confession clearly pointed to Jesus' divinity alongside his humanity. Key texts developing this conviction include teaching from Romans 10:13; Colossians 1:19 and 2:2; also, see John 7:37-40, 8:58, 10:38; Hebrews 1:3; 6:20; and from Revelation 1:8; 1:18 and 22:13.

For further study, I would recommend *Jesus Man of Many Names* by Steve Maltz. This book gives a very good introduction to the person and work of Jesus as it helpfully explores eleven key names/titles given to him. At a more advanced level, I would recommend the book by Richard Harvey, *Mapping Messianic Jewish Theology*, especially chapter 5. See Bibliography (p. 113) for full details.

Question 15

What is Messianic Judaism? Is it a good or bad development?
Also, how should contemporary Jewish believers in Jesus/
Messianic Jews relate to the wider Christian church?

Messianic Judaism, in common with a number of theological terms, is a somewhat slippery one. I offer the following four definitions which I have found helpful:

1) Messianic Judaism is a biblically based movement of people who, as committed Jews, believe in *Yeshua* (Jesus) as the Jewish Messiah of whom the Jewish Law and prophets spoke.[4]

2) Messianic Judaism is a movement of Jewish congregations and congregational groupings committed to Yeshua the Messiah, who embrace the covenantal responsibility of Jewish life and identity rooted in Torah, expressed in tradition, and renewed and applied in the context of the New Covenant.[5]

3) Messianic Judaism is an important and sovereign work of God in which he is not only grafting back some of the original branches but, more significantly, restoring the whole church onto its Jewish root.[6]

4) Messianic Judaism is the movement of Jewish believers in Jesus who affirm that their Jewish identity comes alive in Jesus rather than is terminated by faith in Jesus. Such believers seek to live out their faith in traditional Christological categories[7] and to serve fully as part of the church while seeking to uphold and develop wherever possible special links to the wider Jewish community.[8]

CMJ believes the emergence of the Messianic Jewish movement is part of God's wider redemptive purposes. In supporting the development of Messianic Jews as a recognised people group within the wider body of the church, CMJ believes the Messianic Jewish movement will be a great blessing to the whole church as well as to the wider Jewish community. Clearly there are a number of pressing issues of how various parts of the church relate together in unity, while celebrating God-given diversity and distinctiveness (and such issues often come into focus while exploring the development of Messianic Judaism). CMJ believes it is in a uniquely privileged place of addressing these issues in a biblically faithful and astute way, which will result both in honouring and strengthening unity (Ephesians 2:14-16), while allowing God-given distinctiveness to flourish, in ways inspired by the Holy Spirit.

For further study see my Olive Press Quarterly[9] (Issue 6, 2007) *Root and Branch? Exploring relationship models between the Messianic Jewish movement and the wider church community.* This issue can be downloaded from the CMJ website.

Question 16

'And so, all Israel will be saved' (Romans 11:26). What do you think Paul means by this?

This is a key verse in Paul's magnificent teaching about God's purposes for Israel within the outworking of the gospel.

Let us begin with the term 'and so'. I think it is more helpful to understand the 'and so' as referring to the way in which all 'Israel will be saved' rather than the issue of timing. However, in interpreting this verse it is difficult to be sure if the key idea is about the timing or the method of Israel's salvation. Perhaps both issues are being addressed – certainly these issues are connected and are not mutually exclusive, for Paul wants to declare that the timing of Israel's salvation is clearly different to the majority of the Gentiles who had already, in Paul's immediate context, come to faith in Jesus. Paul in his proclamation of the gospel affirms that the event which results in all Israel being saved is linked primarily to the return (Second Coming) of Jesus. However, while the general timing is different, the method of this salvation will be no different to that of the Gentiles, for the source, content and gift of salvation is the same, namely the person and work of Jesus. The focus, therefore, is on the process of how all Israel will be saved. Paul recognises that in some way the Jewish rejection of Jesus opens up the way for significant Gentile acceptance of Jesus.

This reality is at the heart of Paul's eschatology. Even Israel's predominant rejection of the person and work of Jesus has major significance in terms of completing God's redemptive purposes. This significance is partly shown in that Israel's rejection of Jesus opens up a way, as already stated, for a significant Gentile acceptance of Jesus. This in turn will help to create a new openness in Jewish people, leading to the promise that 'all Israel will be saved'.

Let us now turn to the more substantial part of the verse, namely, '. . . all Israel will be saved.' This statement has been generally interpreted in four main ways. These four ways echo the four possible meanings of the terms 'loaf' and 'branches' (Romans 11:16) in Christian interpretation.

The first line of meaning draws in part, from Galatians 6:16, namely that 'all Israel' means all the elect, both Jews and Gentiles. However, this makes no sense of the way 'Israel' is used in verse 25, and does no justice to the clear contrast between Gentiles and Israel which has been a main theme of Paul's argument outlined in verses 11-32.

The second line of meaning is that 'all Israel' relates to the elect within Israel, namely, the faithful Jewish remnant of Paul's time, alongside Jewish people of future generations who will respond to the gospel. However, this as in the first line of meaning would be stating the obvious and would fail to make any sense of the mysterious hope of some great act of wider redemption, anticipated by the promise of how much greater riches will their fullness bring (verse 12), of their acceptance (verse 15), of the promised grafting in of what had previously been broken off (verses 23-24) and of the irrevocable nature of God's call (verse 29). This line of argument also fails to take into account Paul's 'inclusive' use of 'Israel'.

The third understanding is to see 'all Israel' as the whole nation of Israel, which includes every individual.

The fourth view simply nuances the third: to emphasise the whole nation of Israel does not automatically or necessarily mean every single individual. Clearly this fourth position is in keeping with the way the term is used in 1 Samuel 7:5; 1 Kings 12:1; 2 Chronicles 12:1 and Daniel 9:11. Also in support of this fourth position the Mishnah[10] speaks of 'all Israel' having a share in the world to come, which is then followed by a list of those to be excluded. Overall I prefer to affirm this fourth interpretation of the term 'all Israel'.

Following on from the defining of the term 'all Israel', two further questions relating to the saving of all Israel from the text must be addressed. Firstly, the issue of 'how' this salvation will take place, and secondly 'when' this salvation of all Israel will take place.

In regard to these connected questions, Paul has already presented the view that the saving of all Israel is part of the larger process of God's redemptive purposes, which has included Israel's hardening (9:30; 10:21; 11:26), the establishing and maintaining of a faithful remnant (11:1-6), his own prayer ministry (10:1) and the completion of Gentile inclusion (11:25). Now this process will be completed by the Deliverer who will come from Zion and will renew the covenant and remove godlessness and sin. This Deliverer, in keeping with Isaiah 59:20, could refer to God (*Yahweh*) but, in keeping with Paul's teaching in 7:24-25 and 1 Thessalonians 1:10, it seems here Paul's prime intention is to show the Deliverer is Jesus Christ. While, as stated earlier, the timing is different, the 'process of salvation' for 'all Israel' is not. For such salvation will follow a turning away from unbelief (verse 23) and a calling upon and trusting in Jesus.

I think for Paul both God's judgment and salvation are still not yet fully realised. Paul's eschatology is best not seen as a 'closed book', for it is not an 'over-realised' eschatology. This means that both Paul and his readers (which includes us today!) will need to engage with aspects of temporary uncertainty and present imperfection, as one faithfully works, prays and waits for the full consummation of God's Kingdom purposes.

Question 17

If the restoration of the Jewish people to the Land of Israel is of significance within God's plans, why does the New Testament not say so?

I want to make three main points, in responding to this important question.

Firstly, I do not agree with the assumption in the question that the New Testament does not say some significant things about the restoration of Jewish people to the Land of Israel. For example, in Luke 2:32, Jesus is declared to be '. . . *a light for revelation to the Gentiles and for glory to your people Israel*', and in Romans 15:8 the clear statement is made, that '. . . . *Christ has become a servant of the Jews on behalf of God's truth to confirm the promises made to the Patriarchs*'. Also, in Romans 9:1-5 Paul confirms the ongoing blessings to Israel, which include the covenants. It is extremely unlikely any Jewish person hearing of the glory of Israel, the covenantal promises or the promises made to the Patriarchs would believe the promised hope of the Land and of the future restoration if Israel were not included.

Secondly, the bulk (if not all) of the New Testament was written while many Jewish people were still in the Land, albeit under Roman rule. The final expulsion of Jewish people from the Land took place around AD 135. So at one level it is not mentioned much, as it was not a current pressing issue for them.

Thirdly, as Christians we have a 'Biblical Theology', not simply a 'New Testament Theology'. We accept the whole of the Bible as having authority in shaping our thinking and doing. Jesus affirms this in teaching us that he came not to abolish the Law and the Prophets (Matthew 5:17-18) but to fulfil them. Nowhere in the New Testament do we find a denial of the 'Old Testament' teaching about the Land. Clearly some scholars have argued the promise of the Land has been fulfilled 'spiritually' through the death and resurrection of Jesus. While I understand and celebrate the centrality of Jesus in terms of all Christian eschatology, I am not in any way convinced by the reasoning, which says we should deny or marginalise the clear eschatological focus on the restoration of the Jewish people to the Land of Israel.

Some scholars continue to argue that Jesus 'refocuses' attention away from the promises of the Land. A key verse in this line of argument is Acts 1:6-7. They argue that what Jesus teaches here is that there is to be no restoration to the Land or the Kingdom of Israel. This line of reasoning is, I believe, a popular but serious misinterpretation of the text. In fact what is stated here is that this is not the time for such questions, but now is the time for other work to take place, namely the outreach mission of the church (Matthew 28:19-20 and Acts 1:8). There is no indication from this text that the hope of restoration is revoked or misplaced.

In the light of the vast amount of biblical teaching, it should be affirmed God is working out his purposes through the modern day ingathering of Jewish people to the Land of Israel and that Jewish people have a distinctive role with regard to the ongoing purposes and promises of God.

For further study see *Israel in the New Testament* by David Pawson (Terra Nova, 2010).

Question 18

I have heard you refer to 'Enlargement Theology'. Can you give me an outline of what this theology is?

Any type of theology is simply talking (or thinking) about God and his purposes. Theology is perhaps best understood as the process by which faith seeks understanding. 'Enlargement' is a term I have chosen to explain how the biblical covenants 'change' in response to the person and ministry of Jesus Christ. Enlargement Theology fits into the wider world of Christian theology and especially connects with specific areas within Jewish-Christian relations.

Enlargement Theology also engages with what I understand to be the six key theological areas in which important work must be done if the church is to be set free from a theology shaped by Replacement Theology, in order to develop a biblical, non-supersessionist, missionary-focused and Israel-affirming theology. These six areas are: the Doctrine of God; Ecclesiology (theology about the church); Soteriology (theology about salvation); Christology (theology about the person and work of Jesus Christ); Anthropology; Eschatology (theology about end-times).

I am attempting to present Enlargement Theology as a new theological approach which I hope draws faithfully from key biblical texts (especially Paul's teaching in Romans chapters 9-11), and from a sympathetic engagement with the contemporary Messianic Jewish movement.

I argue that Enlargement Theology provides a rigorous and biblically faithful way forward in contrast with the historically prevalent Replacement Theology which entails the non-biblical assumption (or belief) that the new covenant replaces or supersedes the old covenants[11] given to the Jews. In Replacement Theology the church replaces Israel within God's purposes and the promises given to Israel are either now dead or have been transferred to the church. The historically much more recent idea called Two Covenant Theology holds that God deals with Jews and Gentiles in different ways. In essence it holds that Jewish people are in a 'right relationship' with God through their election implemented through the covenants with Abraham and Moses. This relationship has not and never will be revoked. Gentiles however, are not in this covenantal relationship, but a new and separate covenantal relationship is considered to have been 'opened up' for Gentiles, through the person and work of Jesus Christ. Under Two Covenant Theology these two covenantal relationships are thought to work alongside each other within the purposes of God.

Enlargement Theology is built upon five key foundations. These foundations are known in my earlier book, *The Case For Enlargement Theology*, as 'tenets', and are outlined in some detail (see pp. 181-188 of that book). In summary, they are as follows:

1. God's relationship with the Jewish people is eternal, but it is not static.

2. Gentiles (non Jews) are brought into this covenant through the covenant being enlarged (not replaced) through the person and ministry of Jesus.

3. This enlarged covenant needs to be embraced by all people through faith/trust in the person and ministry of Jesus.

4. The ongoing purposes of God are being worked out today through three different, yet mutually inter-connected communities: (a) ethnic Israel; (b) the church (Jews and Gentiles), and (c) Messianic Jewish believers in Jesus.

5. This threefold understanding of these communities has a creative link to Christian understanding of God expressed within Trinitarian models.

Enlargement Theology is not intended to be a complete theological system, yet it does shed light upon our understanding of God's covenantal faithfulness and the relationship between Jews and Gentiles and the church and Israel. In *The Case For Enlargement Theology* I also deal with questions such as the legitimacy of the church's evangelistic mission to Jewish people, along with the issue of Israel and the Land.

In conclusion, I hope that Enlargement Theology will provide a useful tool within the vital field of contemporary Jewish-Christian relations, and will bring about a significant shift in the understanding of many people, a shift which is based upon a clear application of biblical truth (especially Paul's teaching in Romans 9-11) and a deep appreciation of the importance of the Messianic Jewish movement.

For further study I inevitably recommend (well, I would wouldn't I!) *The Case for Enlargement Theology*. The first three chapters deal with the historical and theological development of Jewish-Christian relations, and in chapter four there is an introduction to the key text, namely Romans 9-11. This is followed in chapters five to eleven with a detailed commentary and analysis of Romans 9-11, with particular focus upon the development of Enlargement Theology. The book concludes in chapters twelve and thirteen, with a presentation of Enlargement Theology and a strong plea that it may be considered carefully, and hopefully may lead to a new understanding (paradigm shift) in Jewish-Christian relations. The book also contains an exhaustive bibliography which suggests to the serious reader many opportunities to explore and reflect at a deeper level.

I also recommend the Olive Press Research Papers (you can download these free from the CMJ website). These papers deal with a number of important theological issues from a broad CMJ perspective.

Question 19

How do you translate James 2:2? Why is this verse such a 'storm centre' of controversy for Bible translators?

Translation of original biblical text is always a strongly contested area as factional viewpoints may entail translation agendas or preconceptions. At the heart of most areas of contention is the issue of meaning. We tend to communicate meaning in sentences rather than in individual words. So to aid the 'correct meaning' of a biblical phrase should we simply translate as far as possible the literal meaning of a word in one language to another language, or should we be willing to paraphrase words in order to aid the meaning for those who will hear or read the translation? Along with this issue, words can change their meaning over time. Should the translator simply ignore this fact and stick to the original meaning of the word at the time it was written, or seek to be sensitive to the new context and make the translation accordingly? These types of questions arise in the translation of James 2:2 especially of the Greek word 'Synagogue'. In verse two the contested word in Greek is clearly the word 'Synagogue' and yet in today's eight most popular English translations, the term 'Synagogue' is not used. It is replaced by either the supposedly more 'neutral' terms 'assembly' (King James/ New American Standard/New King James) or 'meeting' (New International/New Living/ Contemporary English) or, perhaps less neutrally, 'church' (New Century/The Message).

I personally would translate 'Synagogue' as 'Synagogue'. This is for two reasons. Firstly, this is the word James uses – he could have used the term *ekklesia* as he does in James 5:14 as the most generally used term[12] for the gathering of Christians, but on this occasion he deliberately uses the term Synagogue.[13] James here is referring to a group of Messianic Jews who are seeking to oversee Synagogue life and practice in a Jewish way which honours Jesus and clearly expresses faith in him. Secondly, to change the word from 'Synagogue' undermines the 'Jewishness of new covenant faith' and has the potential of robbing contemporary Messianic Jewish believers in Jesus of their biblical identity.

I am not sure why so many translators change the word so significantly here. I fear it may be an example[14] of pre-conceived theological bias 'trumping' good practices in translation. Maybe some translators simply cannot conceive of Messianic Jewish Synagogues or, perhaps even worse, their denominational or theological allegiances demand that they resist such a concept.

Question 20

What is anti-Semitism? Why does it seem to flourish and how should we stand against it?

Anti-Semitism is currently used to refer to 'anti-Jewish' hatred or unreasonable prejudice against Jewish people. However, strictly speaking the term can also mean anti-Arab, as Arab and Jews share a Semitic racial identity specifically as descendants of Noah's son Shem.

The cause of anti-Semitism is a widely discussed and hotly contested question. At one level, it is probably a simple prejudice against the unfamiliar or the distinctive minority within an established community. This prejudice against the unfamiliar, the separate minority, then takes a particular 'shape' and 'flavour' in terms of engagement with various Jewish faith groups. Yet what is such a prejudice rooted in? Is it simply a part of the universal sinfulness of humanity? Such sinfulness echoes in the fear of the 'other' and the mistrust or 'dehumanising' of an 'outsider'. Or is it rooted in something more specific?

Many Christians believe that anti-Semitism is indeed rooted in something more specific than human sinfulness. This specific root is identified within the context of what is often described as 'spiritual warfare' and specific satanic actions. It is understood Satan has always battled against God's people throughout history, from the oppression of the Jewish people by Pharaoh to the massacres by Herod, to the horrors of the Holocaust.

Anti-Semitism has a long and complex history, but in its modern form can probably be traced to pseudo-anthropological social sciences which emerged in so-called 'Enlightenment' circles in early nineteenth century Western Europe. This modern anti-Semitism probably had less of a religious focus (in contrast to the anti-Semitism rooted in

'Christian' theologically motivated prejudice throughout the flawed history of much of the church), for it became more racial in its outworking. Such ideas and methodologies were later developed within Nazi ideology, with horrific consequences.

In terms of standing against anti-Semitism, Christians need to make sure that language, liturgy and theology are cleansed from any anti-Semitic elements. Following on from this we need to take seriously the command of Scripture to comfort Jewish people (Isaiah 40:1) and to build good, supportive and open relationships with Jewish communities wherever possible.

On a personal note, I would also urge Christians to mark Holocaust Memorial Day in an appropriate way each year. We should also be wary of (and alert to) attempts to deny or dilute the truth about the genocide perpetrated against the Jewish race in Europe in the 1940s, by labelling other significant atrocities – no matter how serious they may be – as 'genocide'. We must never forget the horrors which can result from anti-Semitism. We must help the next generation to remember the horrors of history and tirelessly strive to play our part in forming just and compassionate communities.

For further study see Fred Wright, *Father, Forgive Us*. See Bibliography for details.

Ten Bible Talks

Bible Talk 1 Genesis 3:1-15

Heavenly Father, in your Son Jesus Christ is hidden all the treasures of wisdom and knowledge. Touch our hearts and our minds by your Holy Spirit and give us reverence and humility, for without these gifts it is impossible to receive the truth. Amen.

Genesis 3:1-15 clearly deserves the title of a 'key biblical text', for Genesis 3 records the transition from the creation goodness of Genesis 1 and 2 to the reality of human sin, and the consequences of the 'Fall'. The outworking of this sin is seen as the narrative tells of Cain murdering Abel, the wickedness of humanity, the grief of God (Genesis 6:6) and the judgment of God, climaxing in the Flood.

As we turn to the text, we see the reference to the serpent. The serpent is understood either as an image of Satan or as a tool/servant of Satan. The role of Satan and the fall of humanity are reflected upon by a number of other biblical texts, such as Isaiah 14:12-17, Ezekiel 28: 12-19, 2 Corinthians 11:3-14, 1 Peter 5:8, and Revelation 12:9-12 and 20:2-3.

The serpent is presented as crafty and charming. Initially, the serpent is not a slivering snake; this came later as a result of God's curse, as outlined in v. 14. The serpent brings temptation which is both powerful and subtle. And the temptation progresses to a more sinister level (this has echoes with the progression of the temptations Jesus faced, as recorded in Luke 4:1-13). The temptation begins with a simple questioning of God's Word, ". . . did God really say . . . ?" Within this question, a seed of doubt is planted. The seed grows into an open denial of God's Word, ". . . you will not die." From here, Eve desires the fruit of the tree. As this desire is acted upon, deception occurs, and the consequence of sin unfolds.

Within so many of our struggles to respond to God's grace, one is often aware of this repeating pattern of sin: doubt, denial, misplaced desires, and deception. As sin spreads, the image of God within Adam and Eve is distorted. This distortion, I suggest, is seen in three main areas:

Firstly, within human relationships (v. 7).

Secondly, within the relationship between God and humanity (v. 8). In the text, we are given a heartbreaking glimpse of the breakdown of this relationship, with the accompanying loss of intimacy and innocence. Humanity hides as God calls.

Thirdly, within the loss of the fruitfulness and *shalom* of the creative order itself. According to the Midrash of Genesis chapter 3, the rabbis teach six things were lost as a result of human sin, namely: human splendour, human height, length of life, fruitfulness of the earth, the brightness of the stars, and the Garden of Eden.

We rightly acknowledge the loss and consequences of sin. Yet in both Jewish and probably to a lesser extent in Christian theologies, we declare that sin causes the distortion of the image of God within humanity, but not its destruction. Humanity is still 'fearfully and wonderfully made'. Each human life is of great worth and holds a special dignity because of the Creator's image within (Psalm 8). Creation itself despite its decay declares the glory of God (Romans 1:20). I suggest it is of primary importance in our evangelism, pastoral care, and spirituality to hold in a creative tension that all have sinned and are sinners, yet all are enriched by God's gifts, have dignity, and are precious to God.

As the Genesis 3 narrative unfolds, we see God's response. As stated earlier, we see God searching and calling out to hiding humanity. This reality of God's love is displayed in seeking the lost, and is shown repeatedly throughout the Bible and especially, and most wonderfully, within the ministry of Jesus (*Yeshua*). See Matthew 18:14, Luke 15 and Luke 19:10.

In conclusion, let us turn to v. 15. This verse is seen by both rabbinic and Christian teaching as the first Messianic promise/ prophecy within the Bible. Here we have the redemptive hope that the serpent will be crushed. Both Numbers 21 and John 3 develop and connect with this line of teaching. It is also worth noting that the initial human line of the Messiah is through Eve. This is affirmed in Galatians 4:4. This redemptive line is then traced through Seth (4:25), Enoch (5:21) and Noah (6:9) (see also the genealogy in Luke 3).

The understanding of the Messiah's redemption/victory from the curse of (original) sin is fundamental in Christian biblical theology. It is also at the heart of Paul's teaching, for example, in Romans 5:12-21, where Jesus is presented as the new (second) Adam. Such an understanding is liberally reflected in much Christian art and literature. However, for those seeking to share the gospel within a Jewish context it is worth noting that within normative rabbinical streams of interpretation, the 'redemptive' emphasis is not placed on the curse and cure of human sin but rather on human freedom and the call for faithful and obedient responses to God and his Torah, in the light of this freedom. Where this is the case, it raises certain questions around our evangelistic methods among Jewish people (and also among others in a post-modern context), such as the appropriateness of presenting the gospel primarily along the lines of the sinner/ saved paradigm.

May the Lord give us wisdom as we reflect on these things!

Bible Talk 2 Genesis 15

Heavenly Father, in your Son Jesus Christ is hidden all the treasures of wisdom and knowledge. Touch our hearts and our minds by your Holy Spirit and give us reverence and humility, for without these gifts it is impossible to receive the truth. Amen.

Genesis 15 provides special insight into part of God's dealing with Abraham. Here we have a focus upon the establishing of a covenant. The understanding of covenant is fundamental to both Jewish and Christian theology. More specifically, the covenant with Abraham is seen as the foundational and most significant covenant, in terms of 'Old Testament' history and theology.

The covenant with Abraham is one of the five main biblical covenants (the other four being the covenants with Noah, Moses at Mount Sinai, David and the new covenant). The significance of the covenant with Abraham is, as previously stated, foundational to the ongoing life and identity of Israel. In the New Testament, Abraham is seen as a key figure in understanding the gospel. Abraham's faith as declared in Genesis 15:6 becomes a model for faith as explored by Paul especially in Romans 4 and Galatians 3.

God honours this covenant with Abraham throughout his purposes for Israel and the world. This can be demonstrated in three main ways:

Firstly, God brought his people out of Egypt (Exodus 2:24).
Secondly, God sent his Son into the world (Luke 1:72-73).
Thirdly, God has restored Israel to the Land today.

God's dealing with Abraham fits into five main segments in the Genesis texts. Initially we see the calling of Abraham (Genesis 12), followed in Chapter 15 with the establishing of a covenant. Then in Chapter 17 the covenant is confirmed with the mark of circumcision, and this is followed by the birth of Isaac as the child of promise, which is later followed by the testing of Abraham (Genesis 21 and 22). The narrative of Abraham concludes with his death in chapter 25.

Let us turn to chapter 15. In this section, which begins with the calling of Abraham, the covenant is now deepened and enlarged. This process of deepening and enlarging begins with Abraham hearing from God in a vision (v. 1).

Abraham hears three specific words: Firstly, "do not be afraid". This word of reassurance is a recurring theme throughout the Bible regarding those called by God. We see it, for example, in the call to Jeremiah (Jeremiah 1:8), the call to the shepherds (Luke 2:10) and within Paul's ongoing ministry (Acts 23:11). Such words are a challenge for and comfort to God's people to trust him and his purposes. God confirms to Abraham that the outworking of the covenant is in God's hands and that Abraham is held secure within God's redemptive purposes.

F. Payne, in his commentary[15] on this verse sums up Abraham's response to God as someone who is 'helplessly dependent upon God'. There is no way in which Abraham can fulfil God's purposes through his own efforts, but rather the path which is set before him is to be one of dependent trust. The call to Abraham is imparted to him rather than attained by him.

The second word Abraham receives is "I am your Shield". This is a promise of protection. This promise helps Abraham to deal with his fear.

The third word is, "I am your very great reward" – this is a promise for the future. Abraham will have a future legacy to pass on, as a blessing to future generations.

These promises deal with the very things which would have dominated Abraham's thinking. Here Abraham is a homeless man in need of protection and a childless man in need of an heir; here God wonderfully assures him of a future security and future identity. Both of these things are huge issues as Abraham wrestles with the implications of his calling.

The issue of Abraham's need for an heir, for children, is at the heart of the events which follow chapter 15, namely Hagar and Ishmael and the birth of Isaac. The pressing question within this part of Abraham's pilgrimage is: will Abram continue to trust God? – this trust which has been so powerfully declared in 15:6 – or will these pressing needs, these concerns, lead him away from this trust and perhaps to seek to respond to these needs and concerns by his own efforts and schemes, as becomes the case in Chapter 16?

After these words are given to Abraham we see the outworking of the promise, "I am your shield and your very great reward" (15:5). Abraham is called to count the stars, to look up (beyond himself and his own understanding) and glimpse the awesome power of God. The God of creation, the God who flung the stars into the sky. The promise is given that Abraham's descendants will be as numerous as the stars in the desert night sky!

Yet the promise is not simply about descendants, it is also about the Land. Verse 7 states, "I am the Lord, who brought you out of Ur of the Chaldeans to give you this land to take possession of it." The reality of a people, a Land (a place) and a promise is at the very heart of Israel's identity. It is God's gift!

In verse 8 Abraham questions how this promise can be fulfilled. This has echoes in the response of Mary to a similar promise of blessing (Luke 1:34). Abraham's response reveals the strain he was under. A living faith is not fatalism, faith is not facile. Within living faith there can be an attitude of unbelief and questioning which is wrong and leads to rebuke, but equally questioning can be appropriate. Here for Abraham this genuine questioning leads to reassurance. God's grace is at work, a sign will be given to confirm a word to help us in the journey of faith. In the case of Mary the sign is that Elizabeth would have a child (Luke 1:36-37). In this case the sign for Abraham is given through the unfolding of the sacrificial/covenantal ritual.

From v. 9 onwards, God gives to Abraham reassurance by submitting to the covenantal ritual of this period. In verse 11 birds of prey came to disrupt/destroy the ritual and Abraham drove them away. While one must be careful not to draw too much spiritual analogy from the text, many commentators point (helpfully, I think) to the understanding that the birds are symbolic of forces which seek to undermine and prey upon God's people. As God is at work, his people need to be constantly aware of the spiritual warfare they are engaged with and to act accordingly.

In v. 12, we are told the sun was setting, which indicates that from v. 5, when Abraham looks up to the night stars, at least a twenty-four hour period had elapsed. Probably throughout this period, Abraham is reflecting and perhaps 'wrestling' with the implications of the promises of descendants and a Land.

Also in v. 12, the text records that Abraham fell into a deep sleep. This shows that the covenant is God's initiative. God alone makes the covenant, it is not a contract between two equal parties. One party could not contribute because he was asleep.

Finally, in v. 17 a blazing torch appeared and passed between the pieces of the sacrificial meat. This blazing torch/ flame is a sign of God's presence and is found at a number of key occasions in the history of God's redemptive purposes, for example Exodus 3:2, 19:18; 1 Kings 18:38 and Acts 2:3-4.

As one concludes this focus on Genesis 15, there is so much more to explore, but let us conclude by affirming the following three points:

1. Through this covenant, Abraham begins to see God's big picture of promised blessing to all (12:3), a promise which

includes a people and a Land.

2. Through this covenant, we see time and time again the response of faith/trust is at the heart of all true responses to God's grace.

3. God in Jesus speaks similar words to us, words rooted in grace as spoken to Abraham, namely: "do not be afraid"; "you belong to me"; "I am your Shepherd"; "when I call you I will equip you"; "your future is in me", and "no-one can snatch you from My care".

Thanks be to God for his transforming grace.

Bible Talk 3 Genesis 21-22

Heavenly Father, in your Son Jesus Christ is hidden all the treasures of wisdom and knowledge. Touch our hearts and our minds by your Holy Spirit and give us reverence and humility, for without these gifts it is impossible to receive the truth. Amen.

Within this text, we see the unfolding of the promises to Abraham primarily through the birth of Isaac. Isaac is the second of the three great Jewish Patriarchs. It is through these Patriarchs that the covenantal purposes of God with his people become identifiable in history. This point is made powerfully by Blaise Pascal (a 17th century French philosopher) who states: 'The God of the Bible is the God of Abraham, Isaac and Jacob'.

The statement by Pascal is affirmed by Bernhard Anderson, who states:

> This is true in the sense that Biblical faith, to the bewilderment of many philosophers, is fundamentally historical in character. Its doctrines are events and historical realities, not abstract values and ideas existing in a timeless realm. The God of Israel is known in history – a particular history through his relations with Abraham, Isaac and Jacob."[16]

With the birth of Isaac, we glimpse the grace and faithfulness of God (21:1). Paul comments upon the significance of this faithfulness related to Isaac's birth in Romans 9:6-9 and Galatians 4:28-31. In Genesis 21:9 there is in the Hebrew text an interesting play on words: the term Isaac can mean joyful laughter (v. 6) or laughter with a sense of mockery/ malice (v. 9). Perhaps the underlying spiritual issue in the text is: how do we respond to God's gracious gifts, with joy or with mockery?

As the text continues, we see Isaac's pre-eminence over

Ishmael. Yet, God remains faithful to Ishmael. For God hears the cry of Ishmael (21:17), just as generations later God will hear the cry of the Israelites in Egypt (Exodus 3:7). God protects Ishmael and promises him a great future (21:18-20). This reminds us that in God's gracious purposes there is the commitment to bring blessing to all through his blessing to Abraham (Genesis 12:3).

The parting from Ishmael, as he is sent away, is a test for Abraham. Abraham is distressed (v. 11), yet trusts God. In some ways, it can be seen that this testing prepares Abraham for the greater test which follows in Genesis 22. Throughout Abraham's walk of faith there seems to be this recurring theme of 'letting go' – firstly, of his country (12:1), followed by his people (12:1), and then the security of religious practices from his home country and people. Here again, we see a spiritual principle which I suggest is at the heart of discipleship, namely a willingness to let go of our own status/security in order to be open to become what God calls us to be within his purposes.

Following on from the birth of Isaac, we have the account of the treaty at Beersheba. We see here the establishing of peaceful relations with Abraham's neighbours. Beersheba (meaning seven wells or well of oath) becomes a significant place in Israel's biblical history (see Genesis 26:23-33). Also, in modern times (31 October 1917) Beersheba was the setting for arguably the most decisive battle which broke the hold of the Ottoman Empire over many parts of the Middle East. Of equal significance was the hugely significant approval by the ruling Cabinet of the British Government of the text of the Balfour Declaration/Treaty. This approval took place on the very same date as this battle, and the formal signature was added two days later.

As we turn to Genesis 22, the text records the testing of Abraham (and the obedience of Isaac). Here we enter one of the most moving and intense portions of Scripture. The offering of Isaac is full of spiritual significance for both Christian theology and Rabbinical Judaism. In Christian understanding, the offering of Isaac is seen as pointing to the later offering of Jesus the Messiah. There are at least eight parallels between this offering and the offering of Jesus. Let us explore these key parallels.

The first three have to do with issues of relationship:

Genesis 22:2 *Take your son*
Jesus is God's Son – his Son (Hebrews 1:2).

Genesis 22:2 *Your only son*
Jesus is God's only Son (John 3:16).

Genesis 22:2 *Whom you love*
God loves Jesus (Matthew 17:5).

The next parallel explores the place:

Genesis 22:2 *The region of Moriah upon a mountain*
Jesus was crucified in Jerusalem on or near Mount Moriah (see also 2 Chronicles 3:1).

The next parallel is the event:
Genesis 22:2 *Sacrifice him*
Jesus was sacrificed (1 Corinthians 5:7).

The final three parallels deal with details of the sacrifice:
Genesis 22:6 *Abraham took the wood and placed it upon Isaac*
Jesus carried the wood (the cross) for his sacrifice (John 19:17).

Genesis 22:7 The question is asked, *"Where is the lamb?"* Jesus is identified as the Lamb (John 1:29; Revelation 5:6-13 and 14:8).

Genesis 22:13 The Lamb which is provided is crowned in thorns.
A crown of thorns is placed on the head of Jesus (John 19:2).

In addition to these parallels, it is of interest to speculate on the age of Isaac at the time of this event. In Christian art, Isaac is nearly always portrayed as a young boy, but in Jewish art as an adult. This adult picture is probably more in keeping with the text, as Isaac carries the wood, a demanding physical task which implies Isaac was a strong adult in the prime of his life (perhaps even the same age as Jesus was at his crucifixion).

I find these parallels fascinating and faith building. However, perhaps of most importance are the two key differences between the offering of Isaac and Jesus:

Firstly, Isaac did not know what was going to happen (Genesis 22:7), while Jesus clearly knew and told others on a number of occasions what was going to take place in Jerusalem (Matthew 16:21-28). Jesus set his face knowingly and resolutely towards Jerusalem (Luke 9:51).

Secondly, an angel cries out to stop the killing of Isaac (Genesis 22:11-12, 15). The ram then becomes the substitute for Isaac. Yet, there is at the crucifixion of Jesus no substitution and no angelic intervention. Although we know Jesus could have called upon a legion of angels to help him, all we have is silence and darkness from the heavenly realm to accompany Jesus' dying words, *"It is finished"* (John 19:30). Jesus completes his ministry. The most powerful overview of this ministry is given to us by Paul who states: *God made him who had no sin to be sin for us, so that in him we might become the righteousness of God* (2 Corinthians 5:21).

The offering of Jesus for sin becomes central to the gospel message. His death and glorious resurrection (the two sides of the one redemptive action of God) are the core realities of Christian hope. This hope which is rooted in God's faithfulness to Abraham, Isaac and Jacob is made manifest to all who serve the God of Abraham, Isaac and Jacob today through a living trust in the person and work of Jesus.

May the Lord give us wisdom as we reflect on these things!

Bible Talk 4 1 Kings 17:7-24

Heavenly Father, in your Son Jesus Christ is hidden all the treasures of wisdom and knowledge. Touch our hearts and our minds by your Holy Spirit and give us reverence and humility, for without these gifts it is impossible to receive the truth. Amen.

Elijah is a key prophet within the biblical narrative. There are lots of insights for us as we explore his life and ministry.

Elijah is ministering in a time of conflict. Israel is drifting into idolatry. Baal worship is on the rise and there is a severe drought taking place. Israel is a nation under judgment, a nation which has largely turned away from God.

The drought as judgment has a particular resonance as the god of Baal was worshiped as a fertility god – specifically as the god of the rain clouds. Yet Baal was unable to bring the rain and was powerless to break the drought. This reality is reflected upon in a later period by the prophet Hosea (2:8-9).

The name Elijah means 'the Lord is my God'. The meaning of his name is the essence of his message. Elijah is calling the people back to a true living faith in God. This is the challenge which runs throughout his ministry and reaches a decisive point in 18:21. The response to this challenge is recorded in 18:39.

Let us now turn to the text. We are told that the Lord provided for Elijah during the drought and associated famine via a most unlikely source. This was an unnamed widow who had so little she herself was in fact preparing to die (v. 12).

This account shows the astonishing faith, generosity and obedience of the widow. Verse 15 records: *she went away and did as Elijah had told her*. Following this act of obedience a miraculous provision occurs. Such provision has echoes with the provision of the manna in the wilderness,[17] oil for the Hanukah lamp and the feeding miracles in the Gospels.

Yet despite this miraculous blessing, disaster strikes. The widow's son becomes ill and dies. This raises huge questions for the widow as she struggles to understand why God who promised and gave life-sustaining food should also bring death. Is this some random event or God's punishment? (See v. 18).

Elijah does not discuss such questions[18] with the widow but he acts. He cries out to God (v. 20). Elijah ministers to the widow's son just as earlier the widow had ministered to him.[19] Elijah stretches out over the boy and prays three times for his life to return. (Maybe this action of prayer points to the importance of identifying with those to whom we minister alongside the importance of perseverance in prayer?)

In v. 22 the great declaration is made – *The Lord heard Elijah's cry and the boy's life returned to him* . . . . This declaration is at the centre of this event – God is a God who hears the cries of Elijah and throughout history the cries of all his people. God is the God who hears (18:25-29) and acts, unlike Baal. We can see this pattern of God hearing and acting throughout the Bible.

For example:

The first recorded case of people calling out to God is to be found in Genesis 4:26. God responds to this call of faith by blessing the line of Seth which displayed dependence upon God rather than the self-reliance displayed by Lamech.

Abram calls out to God within his response to God's call to him (Genesis 12:8).

The Exodus event begins with God hearing the cries of the opposed Israelites (Exodus 2:23-24).

The Psalmist declares that God hears his cry and acts (Psalm 40:1-3).

Nehemiah calls out to God for help in rebuilding the walls of Jerusalem and God gives him favour (Nehemiah 4:4 and 6:16).

In Romans 10:13 we have the assurance that everyone who calls on the name of the Lord will be saved. For the Lord is the Lord of all and richly blesses all who call on him.

Let us be encouraged by this. Let us strive to honour God and to call out to him with our hopes and fears in the Name of Jesus, Amen.

Bible Talk 5 Psalm 110

Heavenly Father, in your Son Jesus Christ is hidden all the treasures of wisdom and knowledge. Touch our hearts and our minds by your Holy Spirit and give us reverence and humility, for without these gifts it is impossible to receive the truth. Amen.

One of the key principles in interpreting the Bible is to appreciate and explore the 'connectedness' between the gospel and the faithful promises of God rooted in the covenantal promises to Israel. We can see such 'connectedness' at many points, but perhaps the central point for such 'connectedness' is in terms of the Messianic promise flowing throughout the biblical narrative. This promise flows in ways that are coherent, central and continuous.

Let us turn to Psalm 110. In this psalm we see this connectedness in relation to the Messianic promise. However, we also see in the outworking and interpretation of Psalm 110, in terms of its 'Christian fulfilment', a sharp rift between traditional Christian understandings and rabbinical Jewish understandings. Psalm 110 becomes a hugely contested and disputed psalm[20] within the maze of contemporary Jewish-Christian relations; this is summed up by John Proctor, who states:

Here we see contact with the past – a Jewish text, with a tradition of messianic exegesis, but also a far reaching Christian newness. Perhaps nothing better illustrates early Christianity's nearness to yet growing distance from Jewish scriptures and Judaism than its use of Psalm 110.[21]

As we explore Psalm 110 we enter holy ground, disputed ground. On such ground we must learn to tread carefully. The first point which can be firmly proclaimed is that in the period leading up to the time of Jesus, Jewish teachers and scholars clearly taught this psalm should be interpreted as being Messianic. This is part of the Messianic thread running through Scripture,[22] a thread as stated earlier which is coherent, central and continuous. Yet in the light of Christian interpretation of the psalm there has been a reappraisal, largely in terms of a retreat away from a Messianic understanding of the psalm from the rabbinic Jewish side.

This psalm of David is presented in two segments, vv. 1–3 and then vv. 4–7. In the Hebrew text each segment has exactly equal syllables (74 syllables in each segment). This psalm is a coronation psalm, yet the King who is to be enthroned is far greater, far mightier than any earthly king. Within this kingly role there are clear Messianic and priestly dimensions. As one reads and reflects upon this psalm, I suggest there are two striking impressions. Firstly, the Lord alone is the One who gives victory. Secondly, there is a profound unity between the sovereignty of God and that of this 'King' (his Son).

Let us turn now to discover how Psalm 110 is used within the New Testament. I want to focus in on the following four examples:

Firstly, the best known example is when Jesus quotes from this psalm[23] within the context of teaching about the identity or background of the Messiah. The specific question is *"whose Son is he?"* This question is recorded in all three of the synoptic Gospels and provides a key theological ingredient into the events leading up to Jesus' arrest and trial. Let us turn to Matthew 22:41-45 to see the outworking of this teaching/questioning. The context here is one of exploring theological truth. Verses 41-45 are preceded by a range of similar questioning. For example: in 21:23 the Chief Priests pursue Jesus about authority; in 22:16-17 the Pharisees press Jesus about paying taxes/submission to Rome;[24] and in v. 23 we have the arrival of the Sadducees who ask about marriage/resurrection. Yet in v. 41 it is Jesus who initiates the question.

Here Jesus creates the opportunity for a genuine encounter with some key Pharisees.

This question shows that, in the theological climate of the time, Jewish religious leaders saw Psalm 110 as referring to the Messiah. What Jesus teaches here (v. 43) is that the promised Messiah is not simply David's descendant, but is also David's Lord (this insight Jesus says was revealed to David by the Spirit).

The second example is when Peter (Acts 2:29-36) affirms the insight given by Jesus, namely David through the inspiration of the Spirit, understood that his descendant would be resurrected (Acts 2:31) and exalted (Acts 2:33). The result of this resurrection power and glorious exaltation (ascension) is the outpouring in fullness of the Holy Spirit.[25] This reality is what the crowds, to whom Peter is now preaching, are experiencing (Acts 2:33). Such a powerful experience leads the crowds to ask a key question. No longer is the question aimed at gaining understanding, as was the case earlier in Acts 2:12, but rather the question now is about how to make a faithful response – *"Brothers, what shall we do?"* (Acts 2:37). Peter then outlines the steps needed in order to make a faithful response, namely: repentance; baptism (into Jesus); receiving forgiveness and openness to the person and work of the Holy Spirit (Acts 2:38). The text concludes with the news that about three thousand Jewish people accepted the gospel message (Acts 2:41). The number three thousand may well be significant as this outpouring of God's gracious Holy Spirit is the reversal of the outpouring of judgment, which occurs following Israel's idolatry linked to the golden calf, in which three thousand people died (Exodus 32:28).

The third example is when Paul (1 Corinthians 15:20 – 28) refers to the psalm whilst teaching about the significance of the resurrection of Jesus.

The fourth example is when the writer of Hebrews (in 1:13)

quotes from the opening verse of the psalm, while teaching about the uniqueness and greatness of God's Son. Later in Hebrews, the writer explores the priestly ministry of God's Son with reference to Melchizedek (Hebrews 7). This again directly connects to v. 4 of the psalm.

In turning back to the psalm one is also struck by the fierce images of warfare. In some ways this imagery is echoed within parts of the book of Revelation. Such images were the common coinage of kingship in the ancient near-east. The ruler is endowed with power to defeat all enemies. Yet for us in the light of God's Kingdom rule and the victory of Jesus, we are challenged how to interpret and apply such imagery. For us, the victory we celebrate is based not on military might but on the sacrificial death of the suffering servant, his resurrection, ascension and the outpouring of his Holy Spirit. All of this points to an even greater event, namely the return of Jesus, for it is the Lamb who sits as victor upon the throne to bless and reign.

Let us conclude with a prayer based upon the psalm:[26]

Lord Jesus, divine Son and eternal Priest, inspire us with the confidence of your final conquest over evil, and grant us daily on our way that we may drink of the brook of your eternal life, finding courage against all adversities. Amen.

Bible Talk 6
Mary, the Mother of Jesus: A Pattern for Our
Discipleship. Luke 1:26-55

Heavenly Father, in your Son Jesus Christ is hidden all the treasures of wisdom and knowledge. Touch our hearts and our minds by your Holy Spirit and give us reverence and humility, for without these gifts it is impossible to receive the truth. Amen.

As we explore and reflect upon Mary, the mother of Jesus, we enter into the rich mysteries of God, mysteries which surround the beauty of the incarnation and the joy of redemption. We begin by asking the question: who is this Mary?

We know that in Christian art and devotional theology Mary is presented in an immense variety of ways. Often Mary is stylised or idealised in ways which elevate her and the holy family and leave little or no room for the wonder and reality of the incarnation. We will do well to break free from both the distortions of extreme Mariology (the study and devotion of the person and ministry of Mary), and the 'reactionary sidelining' of Mary that is apparent in some Protestant circles (it has been remarked that in some Protestant teaching Mary is relegated to nothing more than a human test-tube). We will shortly turn to Luke 1:26-55, but before doing so it is worth reviewing briefly some of the theological developments and controversies surrounding Mary.

The first controversy is over Mary's relationship to the brothers and sisters of Jesus (Matthew 13:55). It seems from the clear reading of the text that these brothers and sisters are the offspring born to Joseph and Mary (Joseph is probably dead at the time of this incident recorded in Matthew). However, this 'natural' explanation of brothers and sisters is challenged by some commentators with the suggestion that the term 'brothers'/'sisters' is used loosely and can refer to cousins or the brothers and sisters of the children of Joseph from a previous marriage. While it is impossible to rule out such interpretations, they do seem to require some 'robust athletic hermeneutical manoeuvres'! Yet such manoeuvres are necessary, if one is to declare the doctrine of Mary's perpetual virginity.

This doctrine was taught from the late second century and became widely accepted by the fifth century. Alongside the development of this doctrine came the title *Theotokos*, which was given to Mary at the ecumenical council of Ephesus in 431. *Theotokos* literally means 'mother of God'. Later in the history of the church, another doctrine was linked to Mary, namely her Immaculate Conception, which was later endorsed by Roman Catholics in 1854. Mary was seen as a key 'redeemer figure' in terms of reversing the role of Eve in the downfall of humanity (Genesis 3:6) and became the focus of much devotion. The name 'Queen of Heaven' shows the extent of devotion and veneration given to Mary by some. Such devotion is often linked to belief in Mary's 'assumption' and has found expression in pilgrimages to Roman Catholic sites in Guadalupe, Medjugorje, Knock, Fatima and Lourdes.

As a result of such theological developments, Mary the faithful Jewish teenage girl becomes soaked in layers of theological conflict. This theological conflict has rumbled on since the early days of the Reformation and has gained new momentum with the onset of 'Christian feminist' theologies. It is argued by many of these emerging theologies that Mary must be seen alongside other key women of faith (Deborah, Ruth, Esther, Mary Magdalene, Lydia, etc.) as an active faithful woman, who inspires women and serves as a true role model, rather than as a passive idealised religious icon. It is often remarked that the role of passive virginal motherhood is not an easy one to emulate!

Let us now turn away from such controversies and back to

the biblical text, which begins with the foretelling of the birth of Jesus. In Luke 1:26, God sends the angel Gabriel to Mary. Gabriel had already appeared to Zechariah (v. 19) and will later appear to the shepherds (2:9). It is as if God prepares the way for sending his Son into the world by firstly sending the angelic messenger (both here in Luke's birth narrative and in Matthew's account). In Mark's Gospel the preparing of the way for Jesus is the work of a human messenger, namely John the Baptist. The angel messenger is named as Gabriel, one of only two named angels in the Old Testament (see Daniel 8-10). Mary faithfully questions Gabriel's pronouncement (v. 34). This questioning should remind us that questioning can be a key part of faith, rather than an expression of doubt or disbelief. Mary then comes to an amazing state of faithful obedience, one which echoes throughout the history of God's people: *"I am the Lord's servant, may it be to me as you have said."*

The text then continues with Mary's visit to Elizabeth (vv. 39-45). Elizabeth was filled with the Holy Spirit (v. 41) and affirmed and encouraged Mary with her exclamation: *"blessed are you among women, and blessed is the child you will bear!"* Following on from this, Mary sings out her prayer of praise (often known as the *Magnificat*). This song is full of celebration and declaration of God's purposes rooted in his covenantal promises: *"He has helped his servant Israel, remembering to be merciful to Abraham and his descendants forever, even as he said to our fathers."*

In light of this text (and other New Testament insights), what are we told about Mary? How should we see her? I would suggest that Mary is best understood as the first disciple of Jesus. Within her discipleship, I understand there are six important and universal principles relating to all acts of discipleship:

Firstly, a disciple makes open-ended and faithful responses

to God. As stated earlier, the prime example of this is Mary's statement of faith: *"I am the Lord's servant, may it be to me as you have said."* Mary's discipleship begins as she welcomes Jesus into her life. She carries him and cares for him. She also models faith for him. Maybe we should not be surprised that Jesus reflects Mary's faith statement when he himself faces death. Jesus understood the call of servanthood to his Father's will and prayed on the Mount of Olives, *". . . yet not my will, but yours be done."* Like mother, like Son!

Secondly, a disciple needs support. Mary does not try to make it on her own. She finds the support of Elizabeth and later becomes rooted in the community of those following Jesus. I think Mary had a unique empathy with Elizabeth. Who knows what may have become of the vulnerable teenage Mary if she had been unable to stay with Elizabeth for the early months of her pregnancy? (See Luke 1:56). In our discipleship today, we also need the support of others. It is wise to pray that you may find your own 'Elizabeth' – or perhaps you can become an 'Elizabeth' to someone else in need?

Thirdly, a disciple invests in knowing Scripture. Clearly, Mary knows Scripture. The prayer of praise she sings (Luke 1:46-55) is full of Scripture. It resembles Hannah's song (1 Samuel 2), and within her song she draws from Genesis 17, Micah 7 and Job. She also directly quotes from Psalm 34:2 and verse 46, and Psalm 35:9 and verse 47. Later, Mary shows her obedience to Scripture when she and Joseph take Jesus to the Temple (Luke 2:23) for his dedication. Each disciple following Mary's example should invest in the study of Scripture. Such creative study I think demands much hard work, as one seeks to memorise, discuss, reflect upon and, above all, apply Scripture to our lives of discipleship.

Fourthly, a disciple treasures what God gives. Mary treasured Jesus. She also treasured and pondered all the things said about him in her heart (Luke 2:19). She displays wisdom in knowing there is, as a disciple, a time to be open and to tell, but also a time to keep quiet, to hold on to a truth; a time to wait, reflect, refine and treasure what has been given. It is impossible to know how and to what extent the early church was blessed by having Mary's presence and her insights. My own speculation is based on the fact that we know that, later in her life, Mary was cared for by John (the writer of the fourth Gospel). Clearly, John's Gospel does not begin with the retelling of the birth narrative (as is the case in Matthew and Luke), but rather John begins by bringing out the full meaning of the incarnation: *In the beginning was the Word, and the Word was with God, and the Word was God* . . . (John 1:1-2). Where did John receive these insights? My speculation is that they came from conversations with Mary, the first disciple who treasured and pondered the true meaning of Jesus, throughout her life.

Fifthly, a disciple does not take offence. At a number of points during the ministry of Jesus, words are spoken that could be interpreted as potentially offensive to Mary. For example, John 2:4 and Mark 3:33-34. However, there is no record of Mary choosing to be offended in any way.

Sixthly, a disciple perseveres to the end. Mary finishes the course. From John's Gospel, we are told she is at the cross (John 19:25) when Jesus is dying. What love, courage and perseverance Mary, the first disciple, displays under emotionally demanding circumstances. Later, we are told in the Acts of the Apostles that Mary is part of the community of disciples who witnessed Jesus' resurrection and glorious ascension (Acts 1:14). What amazing perseverance blended with courage runs through the course of her life! First, as a young teenager and then becoming a mum, fleeing into exile (Matthew 2:13), returning to Nazareth, watching over Jesus as he grows (Luke 2:52), following him throughout his ministry, watching him die and encountering his resurrection power.

We conclude by stating this Mary is a wonderful woman of God who, as a devout Jewish teenager, entered into the most amazing journey of faith. She was a loving mother, who carried and cared for her child, and who followed the Messiah, holding faithfully to the unfolding revelation of her Son's heavenly mission. Mary, as the first disciple, is one from whom all other disciples can learn so much.

Thanks be to God.

Bible Talk 7 Luke 13:31-35

Heavenly Father, in your Son Jesus Christ is hidden all the treasures of wisdom and knowledge. Touch our hearts and our minds by your Holy Spirit and give us reverence and humility, for without these gifts it is impossible to receive the truth. Amen.

The momentum of Jesus' ministry is building. The conflict is getting starker. Here we have the reported threat from Herod Antipas that he wants to kill Jesus. The context of this threat is that Herod has already killed John the Baptist. Herod's paranoia leads him to fear that John has risen from the dead (Matthew 14:1) and he appears determined to end the ministry of Jesus. Yet at the trial of Jesus (Luke 23:1-25) Herod appears intrigued with him. But this intrigue soon turns to ridicule, as Herod, 'in step' with Pilate, set a course which leads up to Jesus' crucifixion.

It is worth noting the report of Herod's threat was passed on to Jesus by some Pharisees. There is a general understanding that the Pharisees were the most potent opponents of Jesus. While there are strong recorded accounts of such opposition in all the Gospel accounts, this is not the whole picture. For example, in addition to this warning[27] see also the affirmation of the righteousness of the Pharisees in Matthew 5:20 and the individual Pharisee in Mark 12:34, and the statement in Acts 15:5. In many ways, I understand that a strong case can be made that of all the main Jewish religious/political groups active during the time of Jesus (Pharisees, Zealots, Sadducees and Essenes), Jesus in fact shared the most common ground with the Pharisees.

Jesus does not heed the warning. He is not to be deflected from his ministry. He is in step with his Father's will and his Father's timing. All this becomes much clearer as we approach the events which will unfold shortly, namely Jesus' triumphant entry into Jerusalem, the sharing of the Passover meal, his arrest, trial and crucifixion. In v. 32 the reply of Jesus to the Pharisees is similar to the answer given earlier in Jesus' ministry to the disciples of John the Baptist as recorded in Luke 7:21. Jesus will continue his ministry. His ministry deeds will speak for themselves. He will continue to defeat demonic forces and will bring healing. All of this will reach a climax in Jerusalem.

From v. 34 onwards we have a glimpse of Jesus' relationship with Jerusalem. It appears to be a bittersweet relationship. On one hand there is the reality of rejection and consequently judgment, yet this is woven through with the threads of such love, such passion, such longing: *". . . how often I have longed to gather your children together as a hen gathers her chicks under her wings."*

This love, this passionate longing, has echoes of God's love for his children declared time and again throughout the Bible narrative. Consider, for example, Deuteronomy 32:10-12, Hosea 11:1-4 and Luke 19:41-42.

There is to be a real consequence of this judgment: *"Your house is left to you desolate . . ."* (13:35). Will this desolation be the end? Have God's purposes for Israel now failed? Will God turn away forever from Jerusalem? The Bible declares a resounding 'no' to these questions. There is to be a hope and a future. A restoration is promised: *"I tell you, you will not see me again until you say: Blessed is he who comes in the name of the Lord."*

Who is the 'you' spoken of here? Who is Jesus primarily addressing? My understanding is that Jesus is not addressing individual Jewish people (namely residents of, or pilgrims to Jerusalem). For many Jewish people followed Jesus and recognised and served him as Lord. This has been wonderfully true throughout history and into the present. Here Jesus is addressing the corporate – namely the nation and leadership

– of Israel. Here Jesus is speaking to the nation's spiritual focus, the city of Jerusalem. The promised salvation of Israel will only now come when Israel as a corporate entity blesses and recognises Jesus as Lord. This understanding is taken up and developed in the teaching of Paul. For example, Romans 11:26 states,

> . . . *and so all Israel will be saved, as it is written:*

> *The deliverer will come from Zion;*
> *he will turn godlessness away from Jacob.*

In this teaching Jesus links a Jewish national salvation with recognition and welcoming of Jesus at his Second Coming. How you put the details into this teaching is perhaps a secondary task. There is much room for eschatological speculation and the spilling of much scholarly ink! However, what is vital, and what is so close to the heart of the biblical teaching is as follows:

1. God's love for Israel has not been, and never will be, replaced.
2. God's love for Israel will lead to Israel's restoration.
3. Israel's future restoration is inseparable from the person and ministry of Jesus, as Israel's Messiah and Lord of all.

Blessed is he who comes in the name of the Lord!

Bible Talk 8   John 3:1-15 and John 4:1-26

Heavenly Father, in your Son Jesus Christ is hidden all the treasures of wisdom and knowledge. Touch our hearts and our minds by your Holy Spirit and give us reverence and humility, for without these gifts it is impossible to receive the truth. Amen.

The readings from the Gospel of John record two significant encounters. These two encounters are the first recorded by John with individuals who are not part of the community of Jesus' disciples. Both these encounters are given prominence within the text and both appear to be private 'one to one' encounters which are then, later within the Gospel text, made public. John deliberately and carefully chooses to structure his Gospel account in this way; why is this the case? I suggest John deliberately selects these two encounters, to show how the Gospel is for all people regardless of their social/religious background and identity. John chooses these encounters because the central characters are at the extreme ends of society during the time of Jesus.

Let us explore these two central characters. In John 3 we are introduced to Nicodemus. We are told the following: (a) his name; (b) that he is a man; (c) a Pharisee; and (d) a religious leader. This Nicodemus is a 'high status' character, a man with influence and power within Jewish society. In John 4 we are introduced to a character who appears to be the polar opposite of Nicodemus. We meet someone who is: (a) unnamed; (b) a woman; (c) a Samaritan (Samaritans were often in conflict with Jews); and (d) in all probability (due to the fact that she is collecting water alone at midday) a shunned member of the wider Samaritan community. There is a tradition that she was a prostitute, hence the reference to five husbands.

As these encounters develop, we also see major contrasts at work. For example, firstly, Nicodemus came to Jesus. He appears to be in control. He initiates the meeting at night (either out of fear of being seen talking to this 'radical rabbi' or out of a desire to have a full conversation without distractions and interruptions). In terms of the Samaritan woman the opposite is the case. Jesus comes to the woman and initiates the conversation (4:7). The text records that Jesus had to go through Samaria (4:4). This points, I suggest, not primarily to geography (often Jewish travellers avoided the route through Samaria by crossing the Jordan river and taking a deliberate detour) but to a spiritual prompting which shaped the ministry of Jesus.

Secondly, Nicodemus knows about Jesus. He refers to him as rabbi and speaks of his miraculous signs (perhaps referring to the events in Cana in Galilee, or more probably the numerous unspecified events in Jerusalem which took place during the Passover festival (2:23). We do not know if this warm endorsement of Jesus by Nicodemus is genuine respect or some form of manipulative flattery. In terms of the Samaritan woman, she initially knows nothing about this strange man who is talking with her, apart from the fact that he is thirsty and she recognises him as a Jew (4:9).

Thirdly, Nicodemus is presented with a direct personal and theological challenge. Jesus in reply to his opening question, strikes at the very heart of the issue and declares: *"No-one can see the Kingdom of God unless he is born again"*(3:3). In terms of the Samaritan woman there is no direct and immediate theological challenge, but there is a gradual process of questioning which leads slowly to a point of revelation. Also in the case of the Samaritan woman, Jesus shows vulnerability. Jesus shares a genuine need (4:7) with this so called 'powerless woman'. Jesus empowers the weak, while challenging and confronting the powerful!

Fourthly, the response of Nicodemus is left open-ended in John 3. We are not told how Nicodemus responds at this point – while the Samaritan woman's response is known: she becomes an evangelist and enables transformation to take place within part of her community (4:39).

In terms of the challenge to Nicodemus the focus is on the need for a radical openness to the work of the Holy Spirit. The term 'born again' is primarily a description of the transforming work of the Holy Spirit which begins when an individual turns to and trusts in Jesus. This being 'born again' or 'born from above' or 'born of the Spirit' (3:8) points to the redemptive work of God. Such a radical challenge seems to leave Nicodemus perplexed; *"how can this be?"*(3:9) he asks. Yet for Jesus this radical challenge is part of God's redemptive promise and teachers within Israel (see 3:10) should be able to understand this. This promise has echoes within the traditional practices of Judaism which Nicodemus as a Pharisaic leader would have known so well. For when a non-Jew becomes a proselyte to Judaism such a person goes through a process of initiation and is spoken of as being 'born again' as an Israelite. The Talmud speaks of a proselyte as becoming 'like a child newly born'. So Jesus is challenging and inviting Nicodemus to become like one of his proselytes: to start a new journey in which he trusts and follows Jesus. Such a radical journey would demand a costly and humbling new start for Nicodemus and would require the transforming power of the Holy Spirit.

In relation to the longer term consequences of these two very different encounters, we are given some intriguing hints from the wider biblical text. For Nicodemus is referred to twice more in John's Gospel. Firstly, in John 7:50-52 where Nicodemus seems to become an advocate for giving Jesus a fair hearing within the circle of Pharisaic leaders. Secondly, in John 19:38-42 where Nicodemus, along with Joseph of Arimathea, makes sure that Jesus has a decent Jewish burial. This act is seen as an act of great bravery by

Joseph and Nicodemus (all the other disciples of Jesus had already fled) and is probably their public declaration of faith in Jesus. Such an understanding is strengthened by the fact that Nicodemus brought to the burial 75 pounds of myrrh and aloes. According to 2 Chronicles 16:14 this is the requirement for a royal burial. Here, I understand Nicodemus is declaring that Jesus is his King. Perhaps he grieves not only over the horrific, unjust death of Jesus, but also over his previous lack of public witness to him. But even here, when it may have appeared to be too late to make any difference, Nicodemus declares his allegiance! Later (in Acts 21:20), Luke records there are many thousands of zealous Torah observing Jews who have become believers in Jesus. We are not told specifically how they became believers (although we are told that the events of Pentecost began a significant move of the Holy Spirit), nor who witnessed to them, or mentored them in their discipleship. However, let us speculate and affirm that no one would have been better equipped for such a task than Nicodemus!

In terms of the Samaritan woman, we have no more references to her in the biblical text, but in Acts 8 Luke records that the first tentative missionary steps of the early Jewish church were into the area of the Samaritans. Here the gospel is joyfully received (Acts 8:8 and verse 14); again we can speculate that many were ready to receive the gospel for they had already heard the vibrant testimony of the Samaritan woman! (See also *Bible Talk 9* for further reflection on the mission of the church into Samaria.)

If this speculation is correct, then, while these two encounters are very different, they are similar in terms of both having significance and a legacy beyond personal faith. They both impact upon the outworking of the mission of the church – firstly to the Jewish community, beginning in Jerusalem, and then, secondly, into the wider Gentile world, beginning with the Samaritans.

For us today, in reflecting upon these two encounters we declare that the gospel is for all people. No one is too good to need Jesus, and no one is too bad to be beyond his redeeming love and challenging invitation.

Lord, please help us by your Holy Spirit to reach out effectively to all people, to speak their language and to meet them at genuine points of encounter. We thank you for the calling of CMJ, to share the gospel with Jewish people. Please strengthen this part of your work, so all may have the opportunity to hear the gospel, respond faithfully and honour Jesus.

Bible Talk 9 Acts 8:4-39

Heavenly Father, in your Son Jesus Christ is hidden all the treasures of wisdom and knowledge. Touch our hearts and our minds by your Holy Spirit and give us reverence and humility, for without these gifts it is impossible to receive the truth. Amen.

Acts 8 is a key bridge within the outworking of Acts and the missionary efforts of the early church. Here, for the first time, the gospel takes root in an environment beyond Judaism, namely within a Samaritan community and with an Ethiopian man.

The Samaritan mission can be seen as a 'stepping stone' or perhaps as an 'intermediate stage' of mission in terms of taking the church from an exclusively Jewish mission (Acts 1-7) to the wider Gentile world, beginning in Acts 10. The Samaritans were not Jews, but they shared a Jewish ancestry and elements of Jewish heritage. Martin Goldsmith[28] comments on this widening mission context:

> God is gracious and gentle in the way he leads his disciples into new avenues of ministry. He does not parachute them into radical or unacceptable service. Rather he takes them gradually step by step into such untrodden territory. For Jewish Christians at this time to venture directly into mission amongst the Gentiles would have been unthinkable. So the Spirit of Jesus introduces them first to the intermediate stage of witnessing to the Samaritans and the God-fearing Ethiopian.

There is so much wonderful material in this reading. Let me try to focus on the following two major points:

Firstly, I want to focus on the Samaritans receiving the Holy Spirit, and then, secondly, I want to focus briefly on the Ethiopian Eunuch.

In Acts 8:4, we see the gospel is taking root in the lives of many Samaritans, through primarily the preaching of Philip. This is taking place despite strong occult opposition, as highlighted by the person and work of Simon (v. 9). Similar occult opposition is also found in Acts 19. The Samaritans believed and were baptised in the name of Jesus. Yet perhaps the most surprising verse of this section is v. 16, which states: *The Holy Spirit had not yet come upon them*. This is surprising because the normative experience of becoming a Christian as outlined earlier in Acts involved a single cluster of three or four[29] key elements, namely: repentance from sin; faith in Jesus; water baptism and receiving the Holy Spirit. Why now this apparent delay in receiving the Holy Spirit? This delay required the arrival of Peter and John to minister to the Samaritans, in order that they too would receive the Holy Spirit. A number of explanations have been offered in attempting to answer this question:

1. Those baptised were not genuine converts. In fact they did not become genuine Christians until they heard from Peter and John. However, this explanation does not fit in well with the plain reading of the text (see, for example, v. 12). Perhaps this explanation works better for the situation outlined later in Acts 19:2?

2. Those baptised had received the Holy Spirit in the normal way, and therefore what the Samaritans received through the ministry of Peter and John was a secondary filling of the Holy Spirit and the receiving or extension of specific ministry gifts. Such an explanation is advanced by John Calvin and is found in much Reformed theology, but again this explanation does not fit in well with the plain reading of the text. These two explanations deal with the problem of delay, by explaining that in fact there was no delay. Dealing with a problem by denying there is a problem is not very satisfactory, be it in biblical interpretation or in any other aspect of life!

3. The third explanation is to offer the view that this delay is in fact normative. This view proposes that Christian initiation is best understood as a separate, two-staged process: the receiving of the Holy Spirit (often spoken of as baptism in the Holy Spirit) is normally received later after conversion, which is marked by repentance and faith. This view is promoted by many within Pentecostal streams of church life and to some extent (yet drawing from very different theological sources) within Roman Catholic liturgical practice. In both cases the receiving of the Holy Spirit is often linked to a particular ministry (including prayer with the laying on of hands), be it by an anointed powerful Pentecostal leader or in the Roman Catholic context, by someone in priestly orders.

My own understanding is to reject all three of these explanations. I am drawn towards seeing that all Christians should seek continually to be open to new experiences of the Holy Spirit, as Paul teaches in Ephesians 5:18. A Christian should therefore not simply see or seek to limit the receiving of the Holy Spirit to a once and for all experience linked to conversion. I think, however, it is a mistake to insist that a separate two-stage process of Christian initiation is normative. The general tone of Acts and the dominant themes of the rest of the New Testament direct us against this (see, for example: Romans 5:5; 8:9; 8:14-18; 1 Corinthians 6:19; Galatians 3:2; 3:14; 4:6; Ephesians 1:13 and 4:30). I understand what happened here in Acts 8 was something which is best understood as exceptional, and not as normative. Something exceptional did occur, namely this delay in receiving the Holy Spirit. This delay was for an exceptional pastoral and mission-focused reason. The Samaritans were a semi-separate group from the Jewish people and there was much hostility between them. Jesus, for example, shocked many of his hearers by telling a story about a good Samaritan, and also in Luke 9:51 both James and John show their hostility to the Samaritans by wanting God's judgment to destroy the Samaritans. This hostility, like most ethnic identity conflicts, is complex, but can be traced back to the Assyrian invasion of 722 BC. This hostility and separateness between Jews and Samaritans could have resulted in these new Samaritan Christians being forced, or choosing for themselves, to set up a separate 'church grouping' in isolation from the Jewish believers in Jesus. I suggest God chose to withhold on this occasion the fullness of the Holy Spirit until key leaders (Peter and John) could be present. As the boundaries of faith are widening, unity could have been lost in a 'sea of diversity' and cultural conflicts. However, with Peter and John present at the point of the outpouring of the Holy Spirit unity could be maintained and the faith of the Samaritan believers could be properly affirmed and celebrated by the whole church. In the New Testament church, God welcomes diversity but never permits disunity!

It is worth reflecting that Peter, as the lead Apostle,[30] is present every time (as recorded in the first part of the book of Acts) when the Holy Spirit is received beyond the confines of Jewish culture, here with the Samaritans and, perhaps even more significantly, with the first Gentile believers in Acts 10. In Acts 10, Peter is there to declare to the whole church that the Gentiles' faith and initiation into Jesus is valid. In fact Peter explains that the Gentiles have received the Holy Spirit in exactly the same way as Jewish (and Samaritan) believers have. Acts 10:47 becomes a key verse in proclaiming the true unity of Jew and Gentile within the missionary growth of the church. In terms of the cluster of Christian initiation it is worth noting that in Acts 10 the order is different,[31] namely the Gentiles on this occasion receive the Holy Spirit prior to water baptism.

Let us turn now to the second main point, namely the Ethiopian eunuch. In the vast majority of commentaries I have read, this Ethiopian eunuch is seen either as a Jewish proselyte or as a God-fearing Gentile (as is the case in the quote from Martin Goldsmith above). I think both descriptions are false. My understanding is that this Ethiopian is a Jew. This view fits in better with the pattern of Acts in which Gentile inclusion occurs only later in Acts 10.

This Ethiopian Jew is, however, partly an outsider, as were the Samaritans. However, he is a partial outsider because of the teaching of the Torah. For the Torah makes clear that as a eunuch he could not enter fully into Temple worship (Deuteronomy 23:1). It is worth noting here that many rabbis understood that this prohibition would be removed when the Messiah came![32] This eunuch, despite knowing of this prohibition, nevertheless travels to Jerusalem; it is on returning from Jerusalem that God enables him to receive fully that which was previously unattainable to him, through his response to the gospel proclaimed to him by Philip.

Philip, in ministering to the Ethiopian, is a model for so much of our evangelistic work. Firstly, Philip is open and obedient to the prompting of the angel (v. 26) and later to the prompting of the Holy Spirit (v. 29), even when the directions he is given seem strange, namely to go out into the desert. Secondly, Philip initiates a conversation with the Ethiopian (v. 30). Thirdly, this conversation begins at a point where the Ethiopian man is, in terms of both his spiritual searching and his emotional needs (v. 35). Philip engages with the genuine questions and concerns of the Ethiopian. Fourthly, Philip helps him to a saving faith in Jesus and this faith is marked by his immediate baptism.

In Acts 8, we see the ripples of the gospel moving out from the Jewish centre, firstly, to a community of Samaritans and then to a Jewish outsider (the Ethiopian eunuch). Here the gospel overcomes barriers, pointing to an ever greater inclusion which will occur later in Acts 10. For us today, we celebrate that all people can enter fully into Christ when they respond to the gospel. All can fully worship the risen Lord, and all can be filled with the Holy Spirit and experience the effect of his transforming power and presence. Let us respond with a sense of thanksgiving, mixed with awe and humility.

Bible Talk 10 Romans 1:1-16

Heavenly Father, in your Son Jesus Christ is hidden all the treasures of wisdom and knowledge. Touch our hearts and our minds by your Holy Spirit and give us reverence and humility, for without these gifts it is impossible to receive the truth. Amen.

Before we explore this key text, let us focus initially upon the city of Rome. Rome was the centre of arguably the most powerful empire the world has known. As the capital city Rome had spiritual, economic and political power. Clearly, in terms of spreading the gospel the task of establishing a vibrant Christian community within Rome was of huge strategic importance. This importance was recognised by Paul, both in terms of a witness to Rome itself and as a 'stepping stone' to expand the preaching of the gospel further, to the western edges of the empire.

Rome soon became regarded (along with Jerusalem Caesarea, Antioch, Pella and Ephesus) as a key centre for the growth of Christianity. One important aspect in regard to Rome, from Paul's perspective, was that the community of believers in Rome had not been established by him. He was not their founding apostle. So in writing to the community (or communities) of believers in Rome, Paul firstly needs to introduce himself and secondly, and more importantly, to introduce and set out the gospel message which he proclaims. In this way the letter to the Romans becomes a great gift to the church and the wider world; for in this letter we have the most complete, systematic and powerful outline of the gospel. In most of Paul's letters his theological teaching tends to respond to specific pastoral questions arising out of specific contexts or events. He writes as a 'pastoral theologian'. However, in Romans Paul writes more systematically as he outlines the 'gospel of God' (Romans 1:1).

Throughout the history of the church, a case can be argued that when and wherever the message of Romans is heard and applied faithfully a 'creative stirring' is birthed within the church. We see this historically in the first steps of the Reformation, and I suggest we see it today within the field of Jewish-Christian relations and especially in the emergence of the Messianic Jewish movement. For it is in Romans (especially in chapters 9-11) that we have the clearest declaration of God's faithfulness to Israel and the outworking of God's purposes for Jew and Gentile, a purpose rooted in Jesus with a focus upon unity, yet allowing for appropriate diversity to develop.

Let us turn to the text. In v. 1, Paul begins the introductions. He describes himself as a servant/slave of Jesus. He is someone who is called and set apart for the gospel. This 'setting apart' is spoken of in terms of the role of an apostle/emissary. I think it is vital in gaining a true understanding of Paul's calling and gifting, to see his role as an apostle/emissary both as a preacher to the Gentile world and as a prophet to Israel. This dual role is at the very heart of Paul's missionary work. Later (v. 9) Paul develops his understanding of a servant by declaring that he serves with his whole heart. As we glimpse Paul's servant heart, we understand something of his sense of duty and delight within his calling. Such a mixture of duty and delight is what sustains effective long-term Christian service. Duty without delight leads to tiredness and a dead, legalistic pattern of work, while delight without duty tends to lead to a lack of perseverance, especially in times of difficulty, alongside a desire for short-term personal affirmation, rather than to bring the true challenge of the gospel to those around us.

The final aspect of Paul's ministry identity is in v. 11, where Paul speaks with humility of his desire both to impart spiritual gifts and to receive. This 'mutual encouragement' and this mutual dependency in giving and receiving is part of the true meaning of being a member of the community of God's people. We need each other. We need to be open both to give and to receive. The best teachers like Paul know of their need to keep on learning!

In terms of introducing the gospel message, Paul makes three striking points. Firstly, in v. 1, Paul defines the message as the *gospel of God*. This is the theme of Romans. It is about the gospel of God in all its fullness. This gospel is inseparable from the story of God's covenantal faithfulness to Israel. It is promised in the Prophets (v. 2), and it is rooted in the Holy Scriptures (v. 2). It is brought into being through David (v. 3), yet the gospel breaks out beyond the confines of Israel's history, just as the resurrection of Jesus breaks out of the confines of the tomb. The gospel is calling out to people from all the nations/Gentiles (v. 5), and this includes those in Rome. The church becomes the 'called out' community of God.

Secondly, this gospel is the gospel of God's Son (see v. 9). The proclaiming of the gospel is Jesus-centred. This Jesus focus is later developed by Paul and is shown with great clarity in the declaration of Romans 10:9, . . . *If you confess with your mouth Jesus is Lord and believe in your heart that God raised him from the dead, you will be saved.*

Thirdly, the gospel is the power of God, a power which breaks down strongholds, and 'opens up' those who are closed to God, a power working towards the purpose of bringing salvation to everyone who believes (v. 16).

Let us now focus on v. 16. Paul states, *I am not ashamed of the gospel, because it is the power of God for the salvation of everyone who believes: first for the Jew, and then for the Gentile.*

Paul begins by stating he is not ashamed of the gospel. Even in the light of the pomp and might of imperial Rome,

Paul knows of the power of the gospel. It is a power rooted in his own experience. His experience was of a transformation which took him from being a leading persecutor of the church (Acts 8:3 and Acts 9:1 – note here that Paul is known as Saul) to a meeting with the risen Lord Jesus (Acts 9:3-9), to becoming filled with the Holy Spirit and being baptised as a follower of Jesus (Acts 10:17-19).

Paul also knows this transforming power of the gospel is for everyone. This 'universal' context of the gospel is declared again and again in Scripture, for example: *For God so loved the world that he gave his one and only Son, that whoever believes in him shall not perish but have eternal life* (John 3:16), and as Paul himself states, . . . *for all have sinned and fall short of the glory of God and are justified freely by his grace* (Romans 3:23-24). We rightly preach, teach and live out the message that the gospel is for everyone – no one is beyond the reach of the transforming power of the gospel. It is wonderful to hear many messages based on Romans 1:16 focusing upon this universal application of the gospel. However, this is not the only application of the text. A complete application needs also to affirm that this gospel message is first (especially) for the Jew.

This emphasis on 'first for the Jew' shows the un-compromising particularity of the gospel. Gentile faith rests on a gospel rooted in Jewish hope. This is why Paul states in Romans 11:18 that the root is not dependent upon Gentile faith, but rather the root supports Gentile faith. Paul hopes that Gentiles, in recognising the Jewish contours of the gospel, will look in three directions in order to grow in faith: firstly, back to the faith of Abraham; secondly, to the faith of the earliest Jewish believers in Jesus; and thirdly, forwards to the time when 'all Israel' will be saved (Romans 11:26), and all of God's saving purposes for his creation will be fully consummated. It seems clear in Scripture there is a direct link between the return of Jesus and the salvation of all Israel.

I believe the church has a priority calling to share the gospel sensitively and appropriately with Jewish people. A faithful missionary strategy must take seriously the call to the Jew first. Within this, there must be an awareness of the eschatological hope within our evangelistic message. The hope we have is not ultimately in church growth, church renewal or even wider revival, but rather it is in the return of Jesus!

Some argue that this call in Romans 1:16 is now redundant: it may, they say, have been relevant in the time of Paul, but it no longer applies today. However, such a view makes no sense of the context of Romans 1:16. For if we examine the Greek text we can see this verse is written in the present tense. Its application is therefore for every generation. I think there is a clear line of reasoning here, namely that if the gospel is still for everyone and if the gospel is still the transforming power of God for salvation, then it is still for the Jew first.

I think it is necessary for a healthy and mature church to understand God's heart for Israel and Jewish people, to understand, as far as is possible, the beauty of unity within diversity of Jew and Gentile in Jesus. The work that the *Church's Ministry among Jewish People* (CMJ) is privileged to have pioneered in the past, and to maintain today, is a ministry that reflects God's heart for Israel and Jewish people. At the heart of this ministry is evangelism. Some argue the church has abused its evangelistic calling among Jewish people and consequently now has a sad record of misused evangelistic fervour, sometimes even energising the horrors of anti-Semitism. While sadly this may have been the case, we are reminded that the best response to misuse of evangelistic fervour is seldom non-use but instead right use.

In CMJ we seek to share the gospel in a sensitive and appropriate way among Jewish people. We believe that when a

Jewish person responds to the gospel his or her Jewish identity is not revoked but is renewed. Paul, for example, speaks of his Jewish identity in the present tense (Romans 11:1). Sadly, throughout the history of the church, Jewish people were often forced to renounce their Jewish identity before fully entering into the life of the church. May God forgive!

In the earliest church period the question faced by Paul and others was along the lines of, *could a non-Jew become a follower of Jesus without first becoming a Jew?* The answer of the early church was a decisive 'yes' (see Acts 15). This answer was celebrated by seeing that God's purposes were fulfilled by a reconciled people of God, a united people where Gentiles embrace Jewish believers in Jesus without forcing upon them their own Gentile culture, and where Jewish believers in Jesus rejoice in sharing full fellowship with Gentiles. Such unity within diversity is where God is glorified and the transforming/reconciling power of God is experienced.

Sadly, as the pages of church history have turned during the centuries, the reality was that a Jewish believer in Jesus was effectively obliged to renounce his or her Jewishness. The question faced by Jewish people today is the exact reversal of the question faced by the early church. Today the question is: *can a Jew become a follower of Jesus without becoming a Gentile?* The answer again is a decisive 'yes'. The good news is that many Jewish people are indeed hearing and responding accordingly to this 'yes'. What could be more appropriate for a Jewish person than for them to acknowledge and follow faithfully the Jewish Messiah!

The Church's Ministry among Jewish People continues to play a vital part in this process of sharing the gospel with Jewish people and helping to equip the wider church for this key task.

Thanks be to God.

Resources for Further Study

A STATEMENT ON ISRAEL AND
THE PALESTINIANS

A statement approved by Jewish and Arab staff at
Christ Church Jerusalem and unanimously agreed by the
CMJ Council on 22nd July, 2004.

Introduction

CMJ was founded in 1809 by Evangelical Christians who believed that the Christian Gospel, which came from a Jewish context, should be shared with Jewish People as a priority. Its original name: "The London Society for Promoting Christianity among the Jews," though couched in unhelpful terminology, was intended to describe this purpose. The Society also reached out to Jewish People in compassion, providing hospitals, schools, job creation and training for the unemployed as well as teaching and worship in Hebrew.

CMJ believes that the term "Restoration" when applied to the Jewish People is primarily restoration to their Messiah, Yeshua HaMashiach, Jesus the Christ; and secondarily restoration to a safe homeland after 2000 years of persecution. Furthermore, the focus of New Testament eschatology (the doctrine of the end times) is on Jesus and holy living, rather than land. However, the question of what the Ministry thinks about the State of Israel and its relationship to the Palestinians is important – hence this statement.

1. CMJ encourages the Church to express sorrow and regret before God for the dreadful history of Christian anti-Semitism and to renounce all anti-Semitic attitudes. At the same time it encourages the Church to renounce any negative or uncaring attitudes towards Arabs in general and Palestinians in particular.

2. CMJ believes that God has neither finally rejected the Jewish People nor replaced or superseded them by the church. A "remnant" of Jewish Believers has always been included in the church. But what of the majority? Paul teaches that God has a special purpose to bring them to faith in Christ. He writes: "Did God reject his people? By no means". He adds: "Did they stumble so as to fall beyond recovery? Not at all". Paul foretells a future blessing for them, and through them for the world, which he variously describes as "their fullness", "their acceptance" which will be "life from the dead". He concludes: "Israel has experienced a hardening in part until the full number of Gentiles has come in. And so all Israel will be saved…" (Romans 11:1, 11-15, 25, 26).

3. CMJ rejoices in the growing number of Jewish Believers in Jesus, in Israel and throughout the world.

4. CMJ believes that both Jewish and Gentile Believers (including our Palestinian brothers and sisters) are united in the one "olive tree". In fact, Jesus has made Jew and Gentile Believers one "and has destroyed the barrier, the dividing wall of hostility, by abolishing in his flesh the law with its commandments and regulations. His purpose was to create in himself one new man out of the two, thus making peace, and in this one body to reconcile both of them to God through the cross, by which he put to death their hostility". Jews and Gentiles alike are reconciled to God through the cross and "both have access to the Father by one Spirit". Gentiles are "fellow-citizens with God's people and members of God's household …. a holy temple in the Lord … in which God lives by his Spirit" (Eph 2:14-22). There is therefore "neither Jew nor Greek" in terms of standing before God (Gal 3:28). So Jewish (Messianic) Believers in Jesus are not spiritually superior to Gentile Believers.

5. CMJ has never limited its ministry in an exclusive way to Jewish People, nor does it wish to do so. The primary purpose

of the Ministry is to share the love of Jesus with the Jewish People, but it also works for reconciliation between all people (especially between Israeli Jewish Believers and Israeli Arabs, between Israelis and Palestinian; Jewish People and Gentiles) because that is a demand which comes from the heart of the Gospel, for God loves all people equally. This means that he loves the Israelis and the Palestinians equally. God's purpose in creating one new man out of Jew and Gentile is part of his greater purpose through Christ to reconcile to himself all things (Eph 2:15-16; Col 1:20).

6. CMJ does not adopt a position on any particular millennial view, but it has always seen the return of the Jewish People to their ancient land, and on a national scale to their Messiah, as a precursor to the return of Jesus in glory.

7. CMJ rejoices in God's faithfulness to the Jewish People in ensuring their survival as a distinct people during 2000 years of exile and persecution.

8. CMJ rejoices that, after 2000 years of exile and persecution, including the Holocaust, the Jewish People now, at last, have returned to the land from which the majority were dispersed in AD70, although there has virtually always been a Jewish presence in the land. The Ministry affirms: "We see the return of the Jewish People to the land of Israel as a sign of God's faithfulness as revealed in Scripture".

Many members of the Ministry see the return of the Jewish People to the land as the beginning of a fulfilment of covenant promises to them in Scripture. However, it must be remembered that Israel is a secular state which is no more religious than Britain.

9. CMJ recognizes that the State of Israel was set up as a result of a majority vote of the United Nations in 1947 that a Jewish state should be established within Mandatory Palestine and regrets the Arab rejection of this decision.

10. CMJ recognizes the tragic displacement of many

Palestinian people, with all its attendant pain and deprivation, which resulted from the re-establishment of the State of Israel and the subsequent attack on the new state by the surrounding countries. It also recognizes the similar displacement of Jewish People from Arab nations.

11. CMJ understands the determination of the Israeli Jews to preserve the Jewish state, to avoid a return to being persecuted and abused by anti–Semites throughout the world. However the Ministry does not hold any official position as to the appropriate location of the borders of the state.

12. CMJ believes it has a particular calling to show the love of Messiah to Jewish People everywhere. But the Ministry takes the same critical approach to some policies and actions of the State of Israel as it would over any secular state.

13. CMJ affirms that God is a God of justice and peace, and that he desires justice and peace for all people groups.

14. CMJ affirms that God is a God of compassion. We should show that compassion to all innocent sufferers, whether Israeli or Palestinian. The Ministry recognizes that the Israelis, after 2000 years of anti-Semitism, face a resurgence of anti-Semitism, a military threat from various nations, Palestinian terrorism and a threat to the stability of their safe homeland through demographic factors. It also recognizes that many Palestinians have lost their ancestral homes and continue to experience military occupation.

Sometimes they suffer unjustified oppression, humiliation, violence and the destruction of their homes. They also experience economic disaster and lack of infrastructure, partly through Israeli policies and partly through the failures of the Palestinian Authority.

15. CMJ deplores the resurgence of anti-Semitism throughout the world, especially in Western Europe, including the UK, which takes the form of verbal and physical attacks on Jewish People, attacks on synagogues, schools, cemeteries and

memorials, a revival of the world Jewish conspiracy theories, including broadcasting of the (fictional) "Protocols of the Elders of Zion" and even a resurrection of the old blood libel, accusing Jews of ritual murders. The Ministry has always sought to stand with the Jewish People against such evils.

Conclusion

CMJ commits itself to move beyond the present debate amongst Christians, which is often characterized by sterile polarization and inflammatory words, to show understanding and tolerance and to focus on reconciliation, justice and peace for both Israelis and Palestinians. It appeals to mission agencies and the wider church to cooperate in this.

CMJ recognizes the great complexity of the Israeli-Palestinian dispute but believes that the power of God is infinitely greater than this complexity and that we should pray for His sovereign purposes to prevail.

A BRIEF GLOSSARY OF SOME JEWISH, HEBREW AND THEOLOGICAL TERMS

Adonai normally translated as Lord. When stated in capital letters it serves as a substitute for the Tetragrammaton, the ineffable name of God.

Aggadah term referring to all aspects of Jewish life and belief not covered by **Halakha**.

Aliyah literally a 'calling up' often used to refer to the calling to read the Torah Scroll in the Synagogue or the calling of Jewish People to immigrate to Israel, often referred to as making aliyah.

Allusion a method of teaching (used by Jesus) that helps the listener to make connections between different Bible texts and to draw out various insights and conclusions.

Amen liturgical response to prayer in both Jewish, Christian and Islamic traditions. The word has a root meaning in Hebrew of trust (emunah) or truth (emet). Often understood as 'so be it', but a later Talmudic teaching takes the initial letters to represent the term 'God is the faithful King' (el melekh neeman).

Covenant a solemn or binding agreement from the Jewish word 'ber'it' meaning to cut or to bind.

Essenes a Jewish sect active in the time of Jesus with a main community at Qumran. This group had distinctive eschatological convictions and strict understandings about purity and ethical living and produced what is commonly known as the Dead Sea Scrolls. While both the **Pharisees** and the **Sadducees** are mentioned in the Talmud there is no direct mention of the Essenes and it appears they made no direct contribution to the development of Rabbinic Judaism.

Gemara an Aramaic word meaning 'tradition', used to refer to part of the **Talmud** that contains commentaries on the **Mishnah**.

Halakhah term referring to legal (**Torah**) issues in Judaism.

HaShem term meaning 'The Name'. Often used by religious Jews as a euphemism for God.

Hermeneutics term used to describe the method of how the Bible is interpreted and applied.

Historicity term used to describe historical reality. Namely, the degree to which something really happened as reported.

Josephus Jewish historian (37-100AD) who gives unique insight into the Jewish war against Rome (67-70 AD) and into religious and social life within the Roman Empire during the time of the New Testament.

Maranatha An Aramaic term used in Christian liturgy, probably meaning 'Our Lord come' or possibly 'Our Lord has come'. See 1 Corinthians 16:22 and Revelation 22:20.

Messiah English translation of Mashiach in Hebrew meaning the 'Anointed One'. Often in English the term 'Christ' is used, which is from the Greek (New Testament) translation of Mashiach.

Messianic Jews Jewish people who believe in Jesus and follow Him as Messiah and Lord.

Midrash Rabbinic commentaries on the **Tanakh** dating from the second century AD.

Minim term used to indentify Jewish people who are considered to be heretics or outsiders from their own community.

Mishnah literature focusing on the Jewish oral law compiled by Yehudah HaNasi; combined with the **Gemara** to form the **Talmud**.

Monotheism belief in One God. This belief is at the heart of the **Shema**.

Passover from the Hebrew 'Pesach'. A festival to mark the liberation of the Israelites from slavery in Egypt. The last supper which Jesus shared with His disciples is identified as a Passover meal (Seder) in the **Synoptic Gospels**.

Patriarchs the three fathers of the Jewish people – Abraham, Isaac and Jacob.

Pharisees a Jewish sect active during the time of Jesus which flourished from the second century BC to the early second century AD. The Pharisees are often seen as the forerunners of Rabbinical Judaism. Jesus had a 'close association' with Pharisees.

Rabbi a Jewish religious teacher and expert on the Torah.

Rabbinical Judaism the predominant form of Jewish religious life today which has its roots in the development of a post-Biblical Judaism which took place after the fall of Jerusalem in AD 70 and the end of the Temple sacrificial system. Rabbinical Judaism can be seen as a departure, in part, from both biblical Judaism and Messianic Judaism and seeks to develop a Jewish religious life with a central focus upon the Torah (without the Temple) and with a clear rejection of the Messianic claims of Jesus. Today there are three main forms of Rabbinical Judaism – Reform, Conservative and Orthodox.

Sadducees a Jewish sect active during the time of Jesus which claimed a link back to Zadok the priest (I Kings 1). The Sadducees rejected the oral torah and aspects of eternal life as taught by the **Pharisees**.

Sanhedrin Greek term for the assembly of Jewish leaders.

Septuagint Greek translation of the 'Old Testament' completed by the first century BC.

Servant Songs term given to the four songs/poems in the Book of Isaiah in which the servant of God is described (Isaiah 42:1-9, 49:1-7, 50:4-11 and 52:13- 53:12). Christians see the fulfilment of these texts in the person and work of Jesus as the suffering and saving Messiah of Israel.

Shalom Hebrew term meaning peace or wholeness.

Shema Hebrew term meaning hear or listen. The Shema is often spoken of as the 'Jewish statement of faith' or as the most important Jewish prayer as stated in Deuteronomy 6:4.

Sh'khinah Hebrew term meaning the glory of God.

Shul Hebrew term for Synagogue

Siddur Prayer book of Jewish liturgy.

Synoptic Gospels the Gospels of Matthew, Mark and Luke as distinct from the Gospel of John. These three Gospel accounts share common sources and a similar structure.

Tallit Jewish prayer shawl.

Talmud Jewish religious literature which combines both the **Mishnah** and the **Gemara**.

Tanakh a Hebrew acronym for the Hebrew Bible, which Christians commonly refer to as the Old Testament.

Theology talking or thinking about God and his purposes. A process where faith seeks understanding.

Torah Hebrew term meaning guidance or directions, yet mostly translated as law. Also refers to the five books of Moses, sometimes known as the Pentateuch.

Tzaddik Hebrew term meaning a righteous man.

Yeshua the Hebrew name for Jesus meaning 'the Lord saves'. This name is often used by **Messianic Jews**.

Yom Kippur The Jewish festival of atonement.

Zealots a Jewish sect active during the time of Jesus which sought to remove the Roman occupiers from the Land by force. Phinehas, son of Eleazar (Numbers 25:6-15), is considered to be the father of this group.

BIBLIOGRAPHY

Anderson, Bernhard, *The Living World of the Old Testament*, (Longmans, 1958).

Bock, Darrell & Glaser, Mitch (eds.), *To the Jew First* (Kregel, 2008).

Brown, Michael, *Answering Jewish objections to Jesus* (four volumes) (Baker Books, 2000).

Crombie, Kelvin, *For the Love of Zion* (Terra Nova, 2008).

Eaton, John, *Commentary on the Psalms* (T and T Clark, 2003).

Evans, David, *Christians and Israel* (Tahilla Press, 2010).

Fieldsend, John, *Messianic Jews* (Monarch, 1993).

Goldsmith, Martin, *Life's Tapestry* (OM Publishing, 1997).

Beyond Beards & Burquas (IVP, 2009).

Gibson, Richard, *The Unusual Suspects* (Christian Focus, 2008).

Glaser, Mitch, *Isaiah 53 Explained* (Chosen People, 2010).

Harvey, Richard, *Mapping Messianic Jewish Theology* (Paternoster, 2009).

Jacob, Alex, *The Case for Enlargement Theology* (Glory to Glory, 2010).

Jacobs, Louis, *Concise Companion to the Jewish Religion* (Oxford University Press, 1999).

Juster, Dan, *Jewish Roots* (Destiny Image, 1995).

Kjaer-Hansen, Kai, (ed.) *Jewish Identity and Faith in Jesus*, (Caspari Center, 1996).

Maltz, Steve, *Jesus Man of Many Names* (Authentic, 2007).

Newman, Carey, *Jesus & The Restoration of Israel* (IVP/ Paternoster, 1999).

Pawson, David, *Defending Christian Zionism* (Terra Nova, 2008).

Israel in the New Testament (Terra Nova, 2010).

Payne, D, *Genesis/Exodus* (Scripture Union, 1970).

Proctor, John, *Jesus is Lord* (Grove Books [B54], 2009).

Riggans, Walter, *The Covenant with the Jews* (Monarch, 1992).

Sandmel, Samuel, *Judaism and Christian Beginnings* (Oxford University Press, 1978).

Soulen, Kendall R, *The God of Israel and Christian Theology* (Fortress, 1996).

Stern, David, *Jewish New Testament Commentary* (JNTP, 1992).

Wilkinson, Paul, *For Zion's Sake* (Paternoster, 2007).

Wright, Fred, *Father Forgive Us* (Monarch, 2002).

Wright, N T, *The New Testament and the People of God* (SPCK, 1992).

Jesus and the Victory of God (SPCK, 1996).

The Resurrection of the Son of God (SPCK, 2003).

Justification – God's Plan and Paul's vision (SPCK, 2009).

Has God Abandoned Israel for Good? Replacement Theology Examined, Michael Eldridge (Feb 2006).

A New Israel – Supersessionism and Dispensationalism re-examined, Timothy Butlin (May 2006).

Romans 9:1-5 Exploring a key biblical text, Alex Jacob (August 2006).

Israel's role in world mission – The conclusion of God's Kingdom purpose? Tim Price (November 2006).

Root and Branch? – Exploring relationship models between the Messianic Jewish Movement and the wider Church Community, Alex Jacob (May 2007).

Elijah and the Covenant – Implications for Remnant Theology in 1 Kings 19, Frank Booth (May 2008).

Worthless Promise? – An initial response to Stephen Sizer's new book 'Zion's Christian Soldiers?' Alex Jacob (August 2008).

OLIVE PRESS QUARTERLY
(renamed to be Olive Press Research Paper)

Churchill and the Jews – An assessment of two recent studies and their contemporary relevance, Michael Eldridge (Feb 2009).

Sermon for the CMJ Bicentenary service – at Christchurch Spitalfields, 9th May 2009, Bishop John Taylor (November 2009).

A Promise Keeping God – Exploring the Covenants, Israel and the Church, Alex Jacob (January 2010).

The Message of the Shofar – And its applications to Believers through the Feasts of the Lord, Greg Stevenson (November 2010).

Flawed Messiah –The Story of Sabbatai Sevi and Its Significance Today, Michael Eldridge.

NOTES FROM 20 QUESTIONS AND 10 BIBLE TALKS

[1] Hermeneutics is a term used to describe how the Bible is interpreted and applied.

[2] Martin Goldsmith, *Beyond beards and burqas* (IVP, 2009) p. 158.

[3] This view is challenged by another 'Christian Zionist', namely David Pawson (see Bibliography). David Pawson argues for a post-tribulation rapture and promotes what I view as a more classical Christian reformed position in terms of the restoration of Israel rather than what is generally understood as a more dispensational view promoted by Paul Wilkinson. I had the privilege of leading a conference with David and Paul in October 2010 and I think I am somewhere in the middle of the 'reformed/dispensational eschatological spectrum'. I am not sure if this makes me right or just indecisive!

[4] Website statement (mjaa.org) from Messianic Jewish Alliance of America (2005).

[5] Statement from Union of Messianic Jewish Congregations (2004).

[6] John Fieldsend, *Messianic Jews* (Monarch, 1993) p25.

[7] The term traditional Christological categories means that the understanding of Jesus both in terms of his identity and his actions are understood and proclaimed in ways which are affirmed by 'mainstream' Christian teaching— namely Jesus' divinity, his humanity, his sinless life, etc.

[8] My own working definition.

[9] This journal is now published under the name *Olive Press Research Paper*.

[10] The *Mishnah* is the oral traditions/teaching of the rabbis compiled by the early part of the 3rd century AD.

[11] In the Old Testament there are four main covenants. The first, with Noah, is a universal covenant, while the following three are made primarily with a focus upon the Jewish people – namely the covenants with Abraham, Moses and David. Some elements within these covenants are replaced or fulfilled in the new covenant as indicated in Hebrews 8, however most aspects of these covenants are irrevocable as they are given as unconditional promises by God. These remain as part of God's redemptive plan. For a fuller study of these covenantal promises and purposes see The Olive Press Research Paper *A Promise Keeping God* (A full list of all these research papers is given above p. 115).

[12] The term *ekklesia* is used 112 times in the New Testament.

[13] The term 'synagogue' is used 57 times in the New Testament in the context of a gathering/assembly of religious Jewish People. On each occasion it is virtually universally translated into English as 'synagogue'.

[14] Another possible example of this is the translation of Romans 10:4, especially how the term 'end' (*telos*) is understood. For a full discussion on this see David Stern, *Jewish New Testament Commentary*.

[15] Payne F, *Genesis/Exodus* (Scripture Union, 1970).

[16] Anderson Bernhard, *The Living World of the Old Testament* (Longmans, 1958).

[17] There is in rabbinical teaching a strong link between Moses and Elijah. This connection is also affirmed in the transfiguration account in Matthew 17:3.

[18] However, Elijah's words in v. 20 as he cries out to God show that Elijah himself faced similar questions.

[19] I think this mutual sense of ministry is an important pastoral truth. Healthy Christian relationships are built upon the ability of people both to receive and to give, to serve and be served. This mutual interdependence is at the heart of community – sadly often we can get stuck in set roles and become trapped

in acting either as givers or receivers/consumers.

[20] Psalms 2, 40 and 72 are also examples of similarly contested psalms within Jewish-Christian relations.

[21] Proctor, John, *Jesus is Lord* (Grove Booklet [b54], 2009), p. 16.

[22] See commentaries on Isaiah 53 and Jeremiah 31.

[23] See Matthew 22:41-45, Mark 12:35-37 and Luke 20:41-44.

[24] This question was probably not a genuine question, but rather it appears to be carefully contrived, asked deliberately in order to try and trap Jesus (Matthew 22:15).

[25] At the heart of Christian theology relating to the Holy Spirit is the understanding that the outpouring of the Holy Spirit is the gift of the ascended Lord.

[26] Prayer from Eaton J, *Commentary on the Psalms* (T & T Clark, 2003).

[27] It is worth noting that in my reading of the text I see this warning as a helpful positive action by some Pharisees who were concerned for Jesus' safety and opposed to Herod's despotic rule. However, this reading is not shared by all and this may be because their reading of the text is preconditioned by a prevailing anti-Pharisee attitude. For example, the NIV study notes state – 'The Pharisees wanted to frighten Jesus into leaving this area . . . .'

[28] Martin Goldsmith, *Jesus and His Relationships* (Paternoster, 2000) p. 77.

[29] Some commentators see repentance and faith as two separate steps while others argue that 'repentant faith' is better understood as one combined step of response to God.

[30] Peter is often spoken of and pictured as holding the keys to the Kingdom (Matthew 16:19). Keys are used in part to unlock. By means of Peter's ministry (to Samaritans, and then out into the wider Gentile world), people's hearts are 'unlocked', opening them up to the work of the Holy Spirit.

[31] God is a God of order and I think it is important to

recognise the normative three- or four-fold process of Christian initiation. However, God's ways are not fixed and we should be open to recognise and celebrate at times that the order changes – the wind, we are told, blows wherever it pleases (see John 3:8). Our systematic theology must not take precedence over God's sovereignty!

[32] See the promised blessings on eunuchs (and foreigners) in Isaiah 56:3-7.

Also by Alex Jacob

THE CASE FOR ENLARGEMENT THEOLOGY

• What are the failings of Replacement Theology?
• What caused the schism between early Christianity and Rabbinical Judaism?
• What theological tools do we need to engage in Jewish-Christian relations?
• How should we interpret the terms 'Israel', 'the church' and 'God's people'?
• How should we understand and apply Paul's teaching in Romans 9-11?
• How should we evaluate the contemporary emergence of the Jewish Messianic movement?
• How should the "Jewish roots" of Christianity translate into contemporary theological models?
• How and why should Christians share the gospel with Jewish people?

This book develops and explores the theme of Enlargement Theology and provides answers to these and many other key questions in the field of Jewish-Christian relations and Biblical Studies. In this exciting study a new theological model is presented which breaks down the barriers resulting from both Replacement Theology (Supersessionism) and Two Covenant Theology.

For all who are seeking to engage in a biblically faithful and astute way within the field of Jewish-Christian relations.

ISBN 978 0 955179 08 2   272pp   £14.99
available from:

www.glorytoglory.co.uk